WITTGENSTEIN'S *PHILOSOPHICAL INVESTIGATIONS*

Continuum Reader's Guides

Continuum's *Reader's Guides* are clear, concise and accessible introductions to classic works of philosophy. Each book explores the major themes, historical and philosophical context and key passages of a major philosophical text, guiding the reader towards a thorough understanding of often demanding material. Ideal for undergraduate students, the guides provide an essential resource for anyone who needs to get to grips with a philosophical text.

Reader's Guides available from Continuum:

Aristotle's Nicomachean Ethics – Christopher Warne
Aristotle's Politics – Judith A. Swanson and C. David Corbin
Berkeley's Principles of Human Knowledge – Alasdair Richmond
Berkeley's Three Dialogues – Aaron Garrett
Deleuze and Guattari's Capitalism and Schizophrenia – Ian Buchanan
Deleuze's Difference and Repetition – Joe Hughes
Derrida's Writing and Difference – Sarah Wood
Descartes' Meditations – Richard Francks
Hegel's Philosophy of Right – David Rose
Heidegger's Being and Time – William Blattner
Heidegger's Later Writings – Lee Braver
Hobbes's Leviathan – Laurie M. Johnson Bagby
Hume's Dialogues Concerning Natural Religion – Andrew Pyle
Hume's Enquiry Concerning Human Understanding – Alan Bailey and Dan O'Brien
Kant's Critique of Aesthetic Judgement – Fiona Hughes
Kant's Critique of Pure Reason – James Luchte
Kant's Groundwork for the Metaphysics of Morals – Paul Guyer
Kuhn's The Structure of Scientific Revolutions – John Preston
Locke's Essay Concerning Human Understanding – William Uzgalis
Locke's Second Treatise of Government – Paul Kelly
Mill's On Liberty – Geoffrey Scarre
Mill's Utilitarianism – Henry West
Nietzsche's On the Genealogy of Morals – Daniel Conway
Nietzsche's The Birth of Tragedy – Douglas Burnham and Martin Jesinghausen
Plato's Republic – Luke Purshouse
Plato's Symposium – Thomas L. Cooksey
Rousseau's The Social Contract – Christopher Wraight
Sartre's Being and Nothingness – Sebastian Gardner
Spinoza's Ethics – Thomas J. Cook
Wittgenstein's Tractatus Logico-Philosophicus – Roger M. White

WITTGENSTEIN'S *PHILOSOPHICAL INVESTIGATIONS*

A READER'S GUIDE

ARIF AHMED

continuum

Continuum International Publishing Group
The Tower Building   80 Maiden Lane
11 York Road   Suite 704
London SE1 7NX   New York, NY 10038

www.continuumbooks.com

British Library Cataloguing-in-Publication Data
A catalogue record for this book is available from the British Library.

ISBN: HB: 978-0-8264-9263-0
       PB: 978-0-8264-9264-7

Library of Congress Cataloging-in-Publication Data
A catalog record for this book is available from the Library of Congress.

Typeset by Newgen Imaging Systems Pvt Ltd, Chennai, India
Printed and bound in Great Britain by CPI Antony Rowe Ltd,
Chippenham, Wiltshire

CONTENTS

PREFACE

This book is aimed at second- and third-year undergraduates who are coming to Wittgenstein for the first time. It doesn't cover all of *Philosophical Investigations*, but it *does* cover everything in it that you would expect to find in any course on the later Wittgenstein: that is, the criticisms of the *Tractatus*, the material on rule-following, and the material on private language.

I wrote the book in the summer of 2009 but it is based upon lectures that I gave, in the Michaelmas terms of 2007 and 2008, to those Cambridge students who were taking the Special Subject paper ('Wittgenstein') in Part II of the Philosophy Tripos. I am grateful to those students for their comments and questions. And I am grateful to Prof. Michael Luntley of Warwick University for helpful comments on Chapter 1.

Quotations from Wittgenstein use single quotes and double quotes exactly as he does.

CHAPTER 1

CONTEXT

If you are going to get anything at all out of Wittgenstein's *Philosophical Investigations* then you must come to it with some knowledge of his *Tractatus Logico-Philosophicus*. That earlier work is by far the single most important influence upon this later one; for instance, the first 100-odd sections of *Philosophical Investigations* constitute a direct and extended attack upon the central theses and presuppositions of the *Tractatus*. Here I say something about the background and content of that earlier work. The first of these tasks involves a brief discussion of the two most important philosophical influences upon it: Russell and Frege.

RUSSELL

In the late nineteenth century the dominant position on the British philosophical scene was idealism. A crude sketch of that position is this: one can never have direct access to reality itself; on the contrary human experience and thought themselves interpose a sort of distorting lens between us and it, so that one could never know reality as it is in itself but only as it appears to us. This view derived ultimately from the *transcendental* idealism that Immanuel Kant had first stated in his *Critique of Pure Reason* (1782).

Russell rejected idealism; the nature of his alternative view is set out with his usual clarity in *The Problems of Philosophy* (Russell 1912). For anyone who is completely new to this whole area, that book is probably the best place to begin.

Russell thought that we *could* have direct knowledge of reality; the relation by which we achieved this he called *acquaintance* (Russell 1912: 23). In particular that relation connects a knowing subject to the immediate objects of its sensory knowledge: these are not enduring physical objects like tables, mountains, and the like but sensations themselves: colour-patches, sounds, smells, and the like. These Russell called *sense data* (ibid. 4). Acquaintance also connects the knowing subject with universals or concepts like whiteness, diversity and brotherhood (ibid. 28).

He extended this account to the problem of intentionality: that is, the question of how thoughts and language could be *about* objects other than themselves. Russell thought that acquaintance gives the answer: 'Every proposition which we understand must be composed wholly of constituents with which we are acquainted' (ibid. 32). Thus the relation of aboutness becomes that of identity: your thoughts just *are* the things they are 'about'; and they are *your* thoughts by virtue of *your* acquaintance with them. And 'you' here denotes not your body but the non-sensory *subject* of acquaintance, which can however also be its object, since one is probably acquainted with oneself (ibid. 27–8).

But surely many propositions do *not* describe items of sensory acquaintance or universals – for instance, most of one's everyday thoughts or utterances. If, for instance, I have the thought *that Henry Kissinger was an astute diplomat* I am surely thinking about a particular object – Henry Kissinger – with which I am *not* acquainted, since (a) he is an enduring flesh-and-blood object and not a sight or a smell; and anyway (b) I have never met him.

Russell's answer may be presented in two stages. The first stage notes that although 'Henry Kissinger' appears to correspond to some element of my thought – when I think that Henry Kissinger was an astute diplomat – what really occurs there corresponds more precisely to an associated definite description, that is, a phrase of the form 'The so-and-so' (ibid. 28). So the thought that I express in English by the sentence 'Henry Kissinger was an astute diplomat' is more precisely rendered by one of the form 'The so-and-so was an astute diplomat', in which 'The so-and-so' should get replaced by whatever description I associate with 'Henry Kissinger', for example, 'The last Secretary of State in the second Nixon Administration'.

The second stage is to note that sentences containing definite descriptions may themselves be replaced with sentences that contain only expressions for universals. Russell himself provided the manual for making such replacements with his famous theory of descriptions. That theory translates a sentence of the form 'The F is G' into this: 'At least one thing is F, no more than one thing is F, and whatever is F is G' or in formal notation $\exists x \forall y ((Fy \leftrightarrow y = x) \& Gx)$. So the next stage in our rewriting of that sentence, which supposedly expressed a thought 'about' Henry Kissinger, is as follows: 'At least one person was the last Secretary of State in the second Nixon Administration, at most one person was, and whoever it was was an astute diplomat.' All reference to Henry Kissinger has now dropped out; a suitable repetition of these stages will also eliminate all reference to Nixon. The resulting sentence contains *only* reference to universals; and this reveals the true contents of the thought or proposition that the initial sentence so misleadingly expressed. We can thus see that after all that proposition *does* contain only objects of my acquaintance, that is, universals. This process of translating sentences into a form that reveals the true contents of the underlying thought is what Wittgenstein called its *analysis* (TLP 3.2–3.201).

FREGE

The formal analysis of definite descriptions to which I have just alluded would not have been possible without the seminal work of Russell's German contemporary Frege. It was he who introduced what is essentially the same quantifier-notation that is taught to all first-year philosophers and mathematicians to this day; doing so enabled him to give a systematic account of arguments of a complexity that was well beyond the scope of traditional logic. In particular it allowed for a systematic treatment of arguments involving mixed quantification, that is, those in whose formal renditions a universal quantifier ∀ occurs within the scope of an existential one ∃ or vice versa. 'Everyone is taller than someone' is a simple instance of this; so too are sentences in which definite descriptions take the position of the grammatical subject, for example, 'The last Secretary of State in the second Nixon Administration was an astute diplomat.'

Here I should also mention three more of Frege's many important contributions to philosophy.

The first was the distinction between sense and reference. A simple way to think about names is to suppose that they just mean what they *stand for*, or as I shall sometimes say *refer to* or *denote* (cf. PI 1[1]). But 'Hesperus' and 'Phosphorus' were names for the Evening Star and the Morning Star before it was realized that both were identical (to the planet Venus). So the statement 'Hesperus = Phosphorus' appears to be both true and informative. But if the names 'Hesperus' and 'Phosphorus' just mean what they stand for then this sentence appears to be saying no more than what we could learn from the triviality 'Hesperus = Hesperus'. Frege concluded that the meaning of a name was not *just* its reference: it further contained an element called its *sense*, which was some proprietary *way of presenting* its referent (Frege 1892: 57). This sense could be encoded in a definite description, so that the sense that 'Henry Kissinger' carries for me is that of 'the last Secretary of State in the second Nixon Administration'. It is the fact that 'Hesperus' and 'Phosphorus' have different senses that explains the informativeness of 'Hesperus = Phosphorus'.

Now as a doctrine about *simple* names Wittgenstein rejected this view in the *Tractatus*. He thought that ordinary *English* or *German* names could be analysed away via the theory of descriptions as already outlined; and further that any names that survived this process of analysis *would* be simple in the sense of meaning just what they denoted (TLP 3.202–3.203).

But he accepted the corresponding view about *sentences*, for he agreed with the second Fregean point that we must distinguish the referents of its elements from the *information* that a sentence conveys. This informational content is the sense of the sentence; so 'Hesperus = Hesperus' plainly has a different sense from 'Hesperus = Phosphorus' even though the elements of the two sentences refer to the same thing. In the *Tractatus* Wittgenstein identified the sense of a sentence with its truth-conditions: that is, the totality of possible situations that would make it true. (This follows from TLP 4.4.) So even though the two sentences seem to say the same thing about the same thing, 'The last Secretary of State in the second Nixon Administration was an astute diplomat' and 'The person who accompanied Nixon to China was an astute diplomat' actually convey different senses, since there is a possible situation – for example, one where it was Mrs Nixon and not Kissinger who went with Nixon to China – in which the first sentence is true and the second sentence is false. The sense of a sentence is the *proposition* or *thought* that it expresses; it is what we judge to be true when we make any judgement at all.

The third Fregean point was the famous context principle: not to ask after the meaning of a name or any other word except as it occurs in a sentence. What this means in practice is that if we know the meaning of every sentence in which a sign occurs, then we know the meaning of the sign itself – there is no further question to be asked about its meaning. Wittgenstein was in agreement with this in both the *Tractatus* and *Philosophical Investigations* (TLP 3.3, PI 49). In the *Tractatus* he took the constituents of the propositions to be not words but variables ranging over all the propositions that contained them: that is to say, they were *functions* that took as values a range of propositions (TLP 3.313). For instance, the proposition *Brutus killed Brutus* contains the function *x killed y*, a function that takes, for example, the value *Brutus killed Caesar* when *x* takes the value Brutus and *y* takes the value Caesar.

As the preceding discussion has already indicated, some of the most important Tractarian doctrines were either elaborations upon or reactions to certain claims of Frege and Russell. Let us now set those doctrines in their immediate context, that is, the theory of meaning of the *Tractatus* itself.

THE *TRACTATUS*

In the *Tractatus* Wittgenstein was concerned to answer the question of intentionality: how can thought and language manage to be *about* something external to themselves? He accepted the referentialist theory that names mean just what they denote; he was therefore also committed to the Russellian programme of analysing everyday sentences to reveal the thoughts they express as combinations of propositions containing only such simple names as meet this demand.

Several further questions arise at this point. First, what sorts of things did he think that the names of a fully analysed language denoted? Second, how did these names combine to form meaningful sentences? Third, how did these sentences combine to form the sentences of everyday language?

What dictated his answer to the first question was a certain departure from Russell's epistemological concerns. Among Wittgenstein's most fundamental ideas at this point was that our thoughts have a definite sense: each thought exhaustively divides the space of possibilities into those that make it *true* and those that make it *false*. But in order to say anything about such possibilities, there must in all of them be something for the thought to be *about*. So what the names in the thought denote are things that exist in all possible worlds.

> It is obvious that an imagined world, however different it may be from the real one, must have something – a form – in common with it. (TLP 2.022)

These objects – which together constitute the form of the world – must therefore be indestructible. And since whatever is composite could be decomposed, that means that they are completely simple entities. Wittgenstein does not say anything further about their nature in the *Tractatus*; nor does he say whether they are identical to the objects of Russellian acquaintance – though we have no reason to think that they are.

His answer to the second question was the famous *picture theory of meaning*. A sentence consists in an arrangement of names like symbols on a map; *that* two names stand in a relation (e.g. that 'Jane' and 'John' stand to the left and the right of the word 'loves') tells us – truly or falsely – that a certain state of affairs obtains in reality (e.g. that Jane loves John): TLP 3.1432.

According to this pictorial theory of meaning a language can never *say* what its terms refer to without presupposing another one; and if my thought is itself in a language ('that language which alone I understand' – TLP 5.62) then this means that the formal similarity between my language and the reality it describes can never be explicitly grasped. However language itself is in a sense an inarticulate signal about that form: it is as it were the medium through which the world communicates its nature to us. For by figuring in the subject-matter of a language with such-and-such names in it, the world reveals to us that it contains such-and-such objects.

But this is something that can only be *shown*. It cannot be *said* (TLP 4.126). Philosophy itself, therefore, and in particular the doctrine of the *Tractatus*, falls into a kind of nonsense when we try to express it in propositional form (TLP 6.54). Philosophy is not a body of doctrine but an activity.

It is evident how this contributed to the mysticism for which the *Tractatus* is famous. And that there are limits to what can be said was a theme that haunted Wittgenstein throughout his career. In the later work it re-emerges in the treatment of ostension (PI 28–35) and of rule-following (PI 85–7, 138–201). But there is a difference. What was mysterious in the earlier work was located in the hidden nature of reality as revealed by language. But in the later work – and this is why it is so disorienting – it is the everyday that begins to seem mysterious. Let us now turn to it.

CHAPTER 2

OVERVIEW OF THEMES

Four main themes run through *Philosophical Investigations*: the idea that meaningful sentences are combinations of names; the idea that what can be said at all can be said precisely; the idea that meaning and understanding are mental processes that accompany speech and writing; and the idea that we can talk and think about our inner sensational states quite independently of what is going on around us. This section briefly outlines his treatment of each one.

We saw that in the *Tractatus* Wittgenstein had taken thoughts to depict possible situations by combining the names that occur within them. In *Philosophical Investigations* he disputes this view – not directly, but by attacking a much broader syndrome of which it is but one symptom. That syndrome may be called the *Augustinian conception* of meaning, because Wittgenstein begins the work with a quotation from St Augustine that illustrates many of its aspects. He then proceeds to attack these ideas. Perhaps most important among them is the preconception that also underlay the *Tractatus*: namely, that there is one single phenomenon of linguistic meaning and that this demands one single theoretical explanation. We shall discuss his attack on this and other Augustinian views in Section 1.

It may be that languages do not all fall under one pattern but rather that they form a *family* in which *different* similarities obtain between different types of linguistic activity. In that case 'language' would be a family resemblance concept. 'But then calling something a language is not saying anything *definite*!' But who says that every sentence can or even *should* say something definite? The *Tractatus* had insisted that every sentence say something precise – so that its truth or falsity was determined for every possible situation; otherwise it does not express a thought at all. Wittgenstein now argues – as we shall see in Section 2 – that that is such a narrow conception of language and of thought as to be inadequate to most of our actual speech, writing and thought. The apparent crudity of language does not conceal perfectly precise thoughts whose content philosophy may then uncover; indeed it is not the business of philosophy to *uncover* anything at all. We conclude Section 2 with a brief discussion of this picture of the philosophical enterprise.

'Nothing is hidden': Wittgenstein argues in PI that what gives words meaning is not some relation between the simple signs concealed within our language and the simple objects hidden beneath the complexity of the world; it is rather our overt *use* of the words of our actual language. But it can easily seem that this is wrong because it can easily seem that some hidden psychological process *must* accompany the *meaningful* use of words; otherwise what distinguishes our speech from a meaningless if highly structured pattern of sound? Again, when you understand a word for the first time it seems as though what has gone through your mind *then*, and not how you subsequently *use* the word, is its meaning; for otherwise how could the former be what guides the latter? Wittgenstein shows that no such accompanying process *could* be what we want meaning and understanding to be. These passages are apt to produce a kind of intellectual dizziness in the reader, for it starts to seem impossible that anyone should ever mean anything. We conclude Section 3 by separating this feeling from Wittgenstein's own view before isolating what really *is* disquieting about the latter.

We have seen that Russell thought that one could refer to the objects of one's immediate sensory acquaintance; this was something that he had in common with many empiricists. It is very easy to suppose that one could set up a means for doing so that proceeded in complete indifference to one's public use of one's words; so that there might be such a thing as a hidden or internal sphere of meaning that was quite independent of public language. Wittgenstein's famous argument that this is not so is known as the 'private language argument': in Section 4 we shall discuss both it and what it is embedded in: namely, a complete reordering of the intuitive way of distinguishing one's 'inner' sensational life from one's outer bodily activities.

I said that the *Tractatus* idea, that certain truths can only be shown, resurfaces in various particular sequences of PI. That is true; but perhaps its most important legacy is rather the overall effect that PI will have on an intelligent and attentive reader. In a sense nothing has changed: one is inclined to go on acquiescing in ordinary 'commonsense' ways of describing reality, so long as these do not attempt to stray into philosophy. But in another sense *everything* has changed: the whole world seems to take on a different aspect.

But this feature is not something that I can attempt here to analyse or explain; if you want to appreciate it you will have to read PI itself. In any case it probably has as much to do with the power of Wittgenstein's writing as with the quality of his arguments, and of course it is only the arguments that concern me here.

CHAPTER 3

READING THE TEXT

SECTION 1. THE AUGUSTINIAN PICTURE

Wittgenstein begins with the following quotation from St Augustine's *Confessions*:

> When they (my elders) named some object, and accordingly moved towards something, I saw this and grasped that the thing was called by the sound they uttered when they meant to point it out. Their intention was shewn by their bodily movements, as it were the natural language of all peoples: the expression of the face, the play of the eyes, the movement of other parts of the body, and the tone of voice which expresses our state of mind in seeking, having, rejecting, or avoiding something. Thus, as I heard words repeatedly used in their proper places in various sentences, I gradually learnt to understand what objects they signified; and after I had trained my mouth to form these signs, I used them to express my own desires. (PI 1)

He says that these words contain a particular 'picture of the essence' of language. 'It is this: the individual words of language name objects – sentences are combinations of such names' (PI 1).

That 'picture' is common to many philosophical theories of language that differ over both the nature of the naming relation and its objects. One such theory was Locke's; another appears in the *Tractatus*. What all such theories have in common is that they offer *uniform* accounts of the meanings of words and of the sentences containing them. Where they differ is over (a) the *kinds* of uniformity that they impose upon language and (b) the *items* that they treat as the true 'names'.

(a) If one says that the individual words of a language name objects, what is one implying that they have in common? Wittgenstein considers three candidates for this role: (i) that they all have the same *function*; (ii) that they all get *introduced* in the same way; or (iii) that they all mean just what they stand for.

(b) Some theories apply the uniform account to our natural languages, for example, English: they treat *their* expressions as having a uniform function or as being introduced in the same way. For instance, Locke's theory of meaning is that ordinary English words name ideas. Other theories concede that expressions of natural language typically do not have the uniformity postulated by the theory but insist that this unity may be revealed by an *analysis* of such languages. For instance, Wittgenstein had held in the *Tractatus* that analysis would reveal meaningful sentences of English or German to be truth-functional syntheses of atomic sentences, the latter being simply combinations of names (TLP 4.221, 5).

In sections 1–64 of *Philosophical Investigations* Wittgenstein attacks various combinations of the positions described under (a) and (b). Initially he considers natural languages; but from PI 39 onwards he turns to the idea that one might defend some of the theses under (a) by restricting them to 'analysed' languages. We start like Wittgenstein with the idea that all the words of a *natural* language *function* in the same way.

Before doing so it is worth introducing one piece of terminology that appears again and again in the course of the work. Many of Wittgenstein's examples involve very simple languages or linguistic procedures, for example, languages consisting entirely of orders (PI 2), of names for colours on a grid (PI 48), or the procedure of inferring what a man is going to do from his expression of a decision (PI 632). Wittgenstein calls these mini-languages 'language-games'. And he also uses the term 'language-game' for the language together with the actions that are typical causes and effects[1] of its utterances (PI 7b–d).

1.1. Unity of function

At PI 1d he asks us to imagine a man who takes to the grocer's a slip marked 'five red apples'; the shopkeeper takes the slip and

> opens the drawer marked "apples"; then he looks up the word "red" in a table and finds a colour sample opposite it; then he says the series of cardinal numbers – I assume that he knows them by heart – up to the word "five" and for each number he

takes an apple of the same colour as the sample out of the drawer. – – It is in this and similar ways that one operates with words.

What the example shows is how *differently* the shopkeeper operates with the words 'five', 'red' and 'apples'. When he sees the word 'apple' he opens a drawer; but when he sees the word 'red' he looks at a colour sample, and so on. But then what hope is there for a *uniform* account of the meanings of those words? And now look at the much greater variety in *our* operations with words. How likely is it that the words of any language approaching the complexity of English could all get their meanings through a single mechanism?

One of the ways in which Wittgenstein makes vivid the difference between the actual functioning of language and that predicted by some preconceived model of it is to imagine a language to which the latter is adequate. That is what he does in PI 2 (and he later describes it as 'the method of s2': PI 48). There he imagines that:

A is building with building-stones; there are blocks, pillars, slabs and beams. B has to pass the stones, and that in the order in which A needs them. For this purpose they use a language consisting of the words "block", "pillar", "slab", "beam". A calls them out; – B brings the stone which he has learnt to bring at such-and-such a call. – – Conceive this as a complete primitive language.

It is easy to see why one might say of *this* primitive language that all of its expressions were names, if one meant by this that they all functioned in the same way. For their uses are uniform (modulo the objects they denote): B does the same with the referent of 'slab' when he hears 'Slab!' as he does with the referent of 'beam' when he hears 'Beam!', that is, he passes it to A. But that reason for imputing uniformity to the language in PI 2 is completely absent from PI 1d. There is no clear sense in which the grocer does the same with the referent (whatever it is) of 'five' when he sees the word on the slip as he does with the referent of 'red' when he sees *that* word on the slip.

One might of course *manufacture* such a sense. One might insist that the grocer is using 'five' to signify the number five and 'red' to signify the colour red. But that is a merely verbal manoeuvre: saying that in each case the word *signifies* the object does not reveal their similarities but conceals their differences.

> Imagine someone's saying: "*All* tools serve to modify something. Thus a hammer modifies the position of a nail, a saw the shape of a board, and so on." – And what is modified by a rule, a glue-pot, and nails? – "Our knowledge of a thing's length, the temperature of the glue, and the solidity of a box." – Would anything be gained by this assimilation of expressions? (PI 14)

The point of the question is as obvious as its answer.

But then what tempted us into thinking that all words function uniformly in the first place? Wittgenstein thinks that there is a specific explanation: the uniform *appearance* of written and spoken expressions that makes them seem to get their meanings in the same way (PI 11b).

> It is like looking into the cabin of a locomotive. We see handles all looking more or less alike. (Naturally, since they are all supposed to be handled.) But one is the handle of a crank which can be moved continuously (it regulates the opening of a valve); another is the handle of a switch, which has only two effective positions, it is either off or on; a third is the handle of a brake-lever, the harder one pulls on it, the harder it brakes; a fourth, the handle of a pump: it has an effect only so long as it is moved to and fro. (PI 12)

In this analogy words correspond to handles: they all look similar. Thus the word 'red' is written in the same alphabet as the word 'five', it is composed in a linear script, and so on. And the different uses of words, like 'five' and 'red', correspond to the different functions of the handles.

But he also has a general explanation: it arises from a tendency that also drives scientific inquiry, namely, the urge to find a single explanatory theory that unites disparate phenomena. Newton's theory of gravitation is a spectacular example of what that tendency can produce: it explains how quite disparate phenomena (apples falling to the Earth and planets orbiting the Sun) arise from the operation of a single mechanism (the force of gravity). In the present case the disparate phenomena are the many varieties of linguistic expression; the explanatory theory is any that tries to explain their meaning as arising through the operation of a single mechanism (here the mechanism of reference). Wittgenstein thought that philosophy ought not to aspire in this direction (PI 109): we shall discuss the reasons for this in due course (2.3).

How convincing is Wittgenstein's attack? A brief examination of what they actually say will make it clear why his likely opponents on this point are unlikely to find the example at PI 1d very convincing. The most likely response will be that that example gets only a superficial description in the passage in question. There are *inner* activities which accompany or precede the grocer's outer ones, and when we look at the totality of his actions we can see that what he does with 'five' corresponds to what he does with 'red' in just the way that what B does with 'Slab!' corresponds to what *he* does with 'Beam!'

Thus consider Locke's version of the thesis. On Locke's view the primary purpose of words is to name one's ideas (*Essay* III.ii.8) – roughly, private mental images. In general these ideas govern one's application of words to external objects by functioning as templates with which to compare the latter (*Essay* IV.iii.2). If a post-box matches in a certain way the private idea that one associates with the word 'red' then one should apply 'red' to the post-box too. If a fruit matches in a certain other way the private idea that one associates with the word 'apple' then one should apply the word 'apple' to that fruit too. Since Locke applies the same account to number (*Essay* II.xvi), his theory implies enough uniformity in the uses of 'five', 'red' and 'apples' for there to be some point in ascribing them all the same function. For in each case what the grocer 'does' with the word is to compare external objects with the associated idea. This both precedes and explains his application of it to the external object. Nothing in the passages that we have considered has anything to say about any of this.

But Wittgenstein was certainly aware of the point. Indeed it gets raised immediately after the example itself: he has the interlocutor ask – 'But how does he know where and how he is to look up the word "red" and what he is to do with the word "five"?' – one tempting answer to the first question being that he finds the colour on the table that matches the idea he associates with 'red'. But he does not address it any further here. He returns to the thought that comparison with 'ideas' explains the external application of our words at PI 73 (discussed at 2.2.3 (a) (iii)). He attacks the thought that words might be made to stand for the subjects of such comparisons at PI 258 (discussed at 4.1.2).

1.2. Ostension

Another uniformity that philosophers have supposed to exist in ordinary language is that its words are learnt by *ostension*: the person who is teaching you the word points to or otherwise indicates the referent of the word while saying it (PI 6b). Such a picture is naturally associated with the classical empiricist view that every word stands for an object of immediate sensory (or introspective) awareness. But it is also evident in the passage from St Augustine. Wittgenstein's view is that there it is the effect of excessive concentration on a small class of expressions:

> If you describe the learning of language in this way you are, I believe, thinking primarily of nouns like "table", "chair", "loaf", and of people's names, and only secondarily of the names of certain actions and properties; and of the remaining kinds of word as something that will take care of itself. (PI 1)

What do you point to on this theory in order to teach somebody the meaning of, for example, 'if'? Maybe there is an answer to this question (cf. the 'if-feeling' discussed at PI II, vi); but in any case Wittgenstein appears to have a general argument against the thesis that *anyone* might have acquired his *entire* linguistic capability via ostension.

That argument appears at PI 28–35. There, Wittgenstein initially appears to be raising a doubt as to whether ostensive definition is possible *at all*. Suppose that I am trying to teach someone the word 'red'. I point to a tall cylindrical post-box and say: 'That is called "red"'. He might be forgiven for thinking that 'red' means post-box, or tall, or cylindrical.

> And he might equally well take the name of a person, of which I give an ostensive definition, as that of a colour, of a race,

or even of a point of the compass. That is to say: an ostensive definition can be variously interpreted in *every* case. (PI 28)

Nor could I remove that possibility of misunderstanding by saying: 'That *colour* is called: "red"', for the same possibility of misunderstanding will arise when I try to give an ostensive definition of 'colour' (PI 29a). Neither would it help for me to point to several objects (say, a post-box, a fire-engine and a tomato) while saying 'All of these are called: "red".' For the pupil might take 'red' to be a predicate true of all and only post-boxes, fire-engines and tomatoes.

But these examples do not show, and are not intended to show, that there could never be a successful ostensive definition. For the fact that a *possibility* of misunderstanding exists does not mean that the definition was somehow defective in *any* case, that is, including cases where that possibility was *not* realized. The definition is successful as long as it *does* have the intended effect regardless of whether or not it *might* have had another (cf. PI 87b–c). But they *do* show that for an ostensive definition to be successful the pupil must already be prepared to 'take it in the right way' – he must, for example, understand that I meant a *colour* when I said 'That is called "red"' (or, for example, that I meant a property of a surface when I said 'These are all called "colours"').

Now what does this 'taking it in the right way' consist in? Wittgenstein writes:

> Whether the word "number" [or 'colour'] is necessary in an ostensive definition depends on whether without it the other person takes the definition otherwise than I wish . . . And how he 'takes' the definition is seen in the use that he makes of the word defined. (PI 29)

Now the last sentence does not *equate* 'how you take the definition' with 'how you go on to use the word so defined'; it merely says that we can see the former in the latter (cf. 'determined by' at PI 139b, discussed at 3.1; 'exhibited in' at PI 201b, discussed at 3.4.3). But it is clear enough that in general nothing *other* than one's consequent use of the word is relevant to how one 'takes' the definition, that is, what one takes the word so defined to mean; and indeed Wittgenstein *does* make an equivalent equation slightly later in the text in a passage that explicitly connects it with ostensive definition:

> For a *large* class of cases – though not for all – in which we employ the word "meaning" it can be defined thus: the meaning of a word is its use in the language.
> And the *meaning* of a name is sometimes explained by pointing to its *bearer*.[2] (PI 43)

So we take 'how you take the definition' to mean no more or less than: how you go on to *use* the word.

But this interpretation of 'taking it in the right way' is open to an objection. Surely – the objector will say – whether or not the pupil 'takes the definition in the right way' is at best of *causal* relevance to whether or not he *goes on to use it* in this or that way. Surely 'taking the definition in the right way' is an experience *concurrent* with the giving of the ostensive definition. Such an experience might be, for instance, that of *attending to* the colour or *attending to* the shape of the ostended object. So for the pupil to 'take in the right way' the ostensive definition 'That is "red"'' is for him to attend to the colour (and not, say, the shape) of the ostended object *while* the ostensive definition is going on, *however* he then – and perhaps consequently – goes on to use the word.

Wittgenstein makes two replies to this objection.

(i) There is no *one* thing that one does in all cases of 'attending to the colour'. On the contrary there are many different activities that we call 'attending to the colour'. Consider various occasions for dong so: here are Wittgenstein's examples:

> "Is this blue the same as the blue over there? Do you see any difference?" –
> You are mixing paint and you say "It's hard to get the blue of this sky."
> "It's turning fine, and you can already see the blue sky again."
> "Look what different effects these two blues have."
> "Do you see the blue book over there? Bring it here."
> "This blue signal-light means . . ."
> "What's this blue called? Is it 'indigo'?" (PI 33)

Wittgenstein himself emphasizes the fact that one performs different *bodily actions* on different such occasions – screwing up one's eyes, framing the colour with one's hand, and so on – but the examples establish a similar diversity among the accompanying *experiences*.

But whether we are concerned with bodily actions *or* experiences, it is not clear why this diversity matters – particularly in light of Wittgenstein's doctrine of family resemblance (see 2.1). For an objector might reply that there *is* one type of process or experience that occurs in all of these cases: namely, that of *attending to the colour*. The fact that so many diverse processes *are* acts of attention to the colour should not stop us from saying that they all have that in common, any more than the evident disparities between board-games, card-games, ball-games and Olympic games should stop us from saying that *they* all have something in common, namely, that they are all *games* (cf. PI 66). So why could not a whole range of experiences that differed in diverse other ways not all be experiences of attending to the colour? (Just as a whole range of experiences that differ in diverse ways could still be visual experiences of a face. A Martian might see nothing in common among them. Does that make *us* wrong to do so?)

It would strengthen Wittgenstein's case here to emphasize what he says in another discussion of a related topic (PI 171b). For the fact is that on many occasions of 'attending to the colour', *nothing* that one feels could be a characteristic experience of it – indeed one often has no special experiences at all (other than of the colour itself). When you were reading these last few sentences you were presumably attending to the content of the words and not to their typeface. But where were the experiences of *attending to the content*?

If that is correct then the present objection to PI 33 is beside the point: what distinguishes 'taking the definition [e.g. of a colour-word] in the right way' from taking it otherwise cannot be something that we experience exactly in the first case, since no experience is always present in that case. So the important point against this idea is not the actual *diversity*, along some dimensions, of the experiences we have when we attend to the colour: that diversity is compatible with their *all* being experiences of the postulated type. The important point is that one can take the definition in the right way and feel *nothing at all* that even *could* be such an experience.

(ii) In any event Wittgenstein's really decisive point is at PI 34. Suppose that some psychological state or process *does* obtain or occur on all and only occasions of attending to the shape, say. Can't the pupil misinterpret *it*? – So that, for instance, he attends to the shape (i.e. he has that experience) while I say 'This [pointing] is called: "a circle"' and now he treats 'circle' as the name of a colour.

> But suppose someone said: "I always do the same thing when I attend to the shape: my eye follows the outline and I feel . . .". And suppose this person to give someone else the ostensive definition "That is called a 'circle'", pointing to a circular object and having all these experiences – – cannot his hearer still interpret the definition differently, even though he sees the other's eyes following the outline, and even though he feels what the other feels? (PI 34)

This argument illustrates a pattern that appears again and again in *Philosophical Investigations*. It is as follows: in cases where we are tempted to think that a psychological expression, say 'meaning a cube' or 'pointing at the colour' or 'expecting a loud report', names a particular type of inner state or process, just imagine that a process of that type gets accompanied by – or indeed produces – behaviour that is characteristic of some *incompatible* psychological state, say that of meaning a triangular prism, or pointing at the shape, or expecting a quiet report. When we think about these cases we will say that the supposed inner state or process was, after all, quite inessential to the psychological state of which it had seemed the very essence.

So if we reject this temptation, we see that the possibility of their misunderstanding shows not that ostensive definitions are impossible but only that they cannot operate in an intellectual vacuum. They require a certain background capacity on the part of the pupil. And that indispensable background is this: that the pupil must be prepared to respond, for example, to the definition of the word 'red' by using the word so defined as *we* standardly use *colour*-words (e.g. applying it to both or neither of two chromatically indistinguishable objects in the same light).

Wittgenstein summarizes this conclusion as follows:

> And now, I think, we can say: Augustine describes the learning
> of human language as if the child came into a strange country
> and did not understand the language of the country; that is,
> as if it already had a language, only not this one. Or again: as if
> the child could already *think*, only not yet speak. And "think"
> would here mean something like "talk to itself". (PI 32)

If this really is the correct conclusion then Augustine was wrong
to place ostensive definition at the foundation of *all* language. In
order that an ostensive definition be successful the pupil must
already *have* a language of some sort; therefore no finite pupil
can have relied solely upon ostension.

But *is* it the correct conclusion? It is certainly true that in
order to 'take an ostensive definition in the right way' the pupil
must have *some* capacities that he did not acquire by exposure to
ostensive definition. But why must those capacities be specifically
linguistic?

Here is a possibility. A certain kind of animal can mimic
sounds that its elders make; its drive to do so in a given situation
S depends upon the observable similarity already obtaining
between S and those other situations in which it has heard that
sound. Suppose that the sound is the same as the English word
'red'; suppose that on all and only the occasions O when a child
of this species has heard its elders make that sound, a red object
has been conspicuous to all parties. And suppose that in consequence the child utters the sound 'Red' when and only when a
red object is conspicuous to it. Hasn't the child learnt 'Red' by
ostensive definition *without* already being able to do anything
like speak another language? Isn't he now able to do something
that has as much claim to count as a rudimentary *report* (on
colours in his environment) as have moves in the language-game
of PI 2 (conceived now as a *complete* language: PI 6a) to count
as rudimentary *orders*?[3]

Of course the child would have to come to the learning situation
equipped with capacities that ostensive definition could *not* give it.
In particular it would have to come pre-equipped with a *similarity
metric*. That is, it would have to have been true of it all along that
given any situation S in which a red object was conspicuously

present and any situation T in which only a blue one was, it classed S as more similar than T to the learning situation O in which 'red' got introduced to it. But there is no reason to suppose that this is impossible. Indeed the fact that animals and children as well as human adults make *inductive inferences* in some directions and not others shows that *some* such metric is widespread. For instance, somebody who burns his hand in the fire will thereafter avoid *fire* and not, say, cats: this shows that in some sense he treats subsequently encountered fires as more similar than subsequently encountered cats to the initial fire. Moreover it shows that such a metric is prelinguistic: one *could* have it – and animals *do* have it – in the absence of any language at all.

In short the objection to Wittgenstein is this: why can't the similarity metric that we need anyway for inductive inference be a *non*-linguistic basis for our 'taking ostensive definitions right'?[4] And if it is, then couldn't there in principle be a language-game all of whose terms were taught, and learnt, by this primitive form of ostension?

Now it is true that plenty of expressions in *our* language neither are nor could be learnt by ostension without some further *linguistic* capacities. Theoretical terms like 'electric charge', 'mass', 'inflation' and even 'solidity' are good examples: no *mere* perceptual encounter with, for example, a solid body could impart to me the physical theory in which the concept of solidity finds a place (cf. Evans 1980: 269–70). And it is plausible that speaking a language *is* a necessary condition on possessing that sort of theoretical background. But it is an empirical fact that our language contains terms of this sort and not *only* the sort of term that could be learnt by ostension by someone who has no language; and the argument that terms of the former sort cannot be learnt by ostension is quite different from Wittgenstein's. It therefore seems to me that Wittgenstein has failed to establish the anti-Augustinian conclusion advertised at PI 32 and quoted above.[5]

1.3. Referentialism

A third kind of uniformity that 'all words are names' might seem to impose upon language is this: that all words refer to objects; and the object exhausts the meaning of the word, so that two words that have the same reference *ipso facto* have the same meaning. And if a word has no bearer then it has no meaning.

1.3.1. In ordinary language
Taken as a doctrine about ordinary language this is as clearly false as any doctrine in the area. The first example that Wittgenstein directs against it is as follows:

> Let us first discuss *this* point of the argument: that a word has no meaning if nothing corresponds to it. – It is important to note that the word "meaning" is being used illicitly if it is used to signify the thing that 'corresponds' to the word. That is to confound the meaning of the name with the *bearer* of the name. When Mr N. N. dies one says that the bearer of the name dies, not that the meaning dies. And it would be nonsensical to say that, for if the name ceased to have meaning it would make no sense to say "Mr N. N. is dead." (PI 40)

As it stands the argument might seem too hasty: it assumes that the relation of reference – unlike, say, the relations of precedence or causation – can only hold between a name and something that exists contemporaneously with it. For if we drop that assumption we can say that 'N. N.' continues to refer to N. N. even after the latter has died, and so somebody who thinks that the meaning of 'N. N.' is the object that it denotes can maintain that 'Mr N. N. is dead' remains meaningful after becoming true.

A further example that gets around this objection exploits a refinement of the primitive builders' language-game as it appeared in PI 2. We are to imagine that 'the tools A uses in building bear certain marks. When A shews his assistant such a mark, he brings the tool that has that mark on it' (PI 15). These marks may be regarded as the names of the objects that bear them.

> But has for instance a name which has *never* been used for a tool also got a meaning in that game? – – Let us assume that "X" is such a sign and that A gives this sign to B – well, even such signs could be given a place in the language-game, and B might have, say, to answer them too with a shake of the head. (One could imagine this as a sort of joke between them.) (PI 42)

Even the name 'X' has *some* sort of meaning; but not only *is* there not anything to be its bearer (as is true also of 'Mr N. N.'): there *never was*. And it is very easy to imagine names and other expressions of ordinary language that clearly have as much use as 'X', and which equally clearly have no bearers (e.g. names from fiction like 'Sherlock Holmes', or names like 'Atlantis' and 'Vulcan' that are associated with conditions that turned out to be unsatisfied). It is therefore false that bearerless expressions of *ordinary* language are meaningless.

1.3.2. In the Tractatus

But another application of this doctrine is not to ordinary language but to what in the *Tractatus* Wittgenstein had called its 'analysis'. Wittgenstein then believed that thoughts made a determinate claim about reality: this means that if I have a thought, say that Napoleon conquered Russia in 1812, *every* possible situation makes that thought *either* true *or* false. But how can this be? After all Napoleon might never have lived (if, for example, his parents had never met). So how, in a possible situation where he never *did* live, could my thought be so much as a *thought* – let alone true or false – if there is nothing there (i.e. no Napoleon) for it to be *about*?

In the *Tractatus* his answer had been that the universe consists of *objects* (TLP 2.021). The possible *configurations* of these objects exhaust *all* possibilities: every possibility for our world is therefore one where all actual objects exist (TLP 2.022–2.023, 2.0271). Those objects are therefore indestructible, that is, necessarily existent; since all that is composite might be decomposed, it follows that the objects are *simple* (TLP 2.02). A thought describes a possibility by describing some possible configuration of simple objects: these possible configurations are *states of affairs* (TLP 2.0272). A thought describes a state of affairs in an essentially pictorial manner (TLP 2.1, 3). It consists of *names* for the objects that figure in that state of affairs (TLP 3.202); the name simply means what it refers to (TLP 3.203); and the *configuration* of names depicts the possible configuration of the objects named (TLP 3.21).

Our initial question was how could my (false) thought, that Napoleon conquered Russia in 1812, be so much as a *thought* about possible situations in which Napoleon never existed – in which, therefore, there is apparently nothing *for* it to *be* about? And the answer is that the thought is really not about Napoleon; or if you like that it *is* about him, but only by virtue of being about those simple and indestructible objects of which he is composed. Those objects exist in all possible situations; it is only that in ones where they have certain arrangements Napoleon himself does *not* exist. So there is always something for my thought to be true about; that is why it can be true or false of *every* possible situation.

In order to apply this account to everyday languages Wittgenstein proposed that those languages in fact conceal the structure of the thoughts that we use them to express (TLP 4.002); what *they* present as simple ('Napoleon') are really objects of great complexity. It is only through the *analysis* of ordinary language that we may reveal the perfectly precise content of those thoughts; so that the elements of a fully analysed sentence correspond to those of a thought (TLP 3.2–3.201).

For instance, sentences of ordinary language contain simple elements that appear to name entities that are complex and hence destructible. For example, 'Cleopatra's Needle' appears to name a large and complex object that might one day cease to exist and in any event might never have existed. (Note that 'Cleopatra's Needle' is not a description but a name: what it denotes is not a needle and was never Cleopatra's.) So a sentence such as 'Cleopatra's Needle is made from granite' does not mirror the structure of the thoughts it expresses. Full analysis of it will reveal a simple sentence, or a complex combination of simple sentences, in which names of simple and hence indestructible objects are combined in a way that depicts a possible combination of those objects.

To pursue this example for merely illustrative purposes: 'Cleopatra's needle is made from granite' might get rendered as '$N_1 N_2 N_3 \ldots N_k G$'. Here 'N_1' ... 'N_k' names the atoms that compose Cleopatra's needle; G names the relation that atoms stand in when they compose something granite; and the concatenation of names of atoms on the left with that of a universal on the right is a way of saying that the universal applies to the atoms (cf. TLP 3.1432).

This example is more definite than the *Tractatus* ever was about the kind of sentence that analysis ultimately reveals.

But independently of that, it does illustrate the crucial point that what appear to be names in ordinary language get eliminated in analysis: 'Cleopatra's Needle' has vanished altogether from '$N_1N_2N_3 \ldots N_kG$'. This gave Wittgenstein room in the earlier work to maintain that all the elements of analysed sentences are expressions that mean exactly what they denote (what he there called 'names') while conceding that this was not so for everyday, or unanalysed language. For only the latter contains expressions like 'Cleopatra's Needle' or 'Mr N. N.', that is, ones that mean something whether or not their referents exist. Whereas the elements of a fully analysed language, like 'N_3' or 'G', refer only to what *could not have failed* to exist.

We shall focus upon two points that Wittgenstein now makes against his earlier position. First, he questions the very intelligibility of the idea that the world is made up of absolutely simple objects; second, he denies that the analysed version of an ordinary-language sentence expresses the *same* meaning *more* perspicuously. We shall consider these in turn.

1.3.3. Simplicity

Wittgenstein says that it makes no sense to speak *absolutely* of simplicity and compositeness:

> What are the simple constituent parts of a chair? – The bits of wood from which it is made? Or the molecules, or the atoms? – "Simple" means: not composite. And here the point is: in what sense 'composite'? It makes no sense at all to speak absolutely of the 'simple parts of a chair' . . . But isn't a chessboard, for instance, obviously, and absolutely, composite? – You are probably thinking of the composition out of thirty-two white and thirty-two black squares. But could we not also say, for instance, that it was composed of the colours black and white and the schema of squares? And if there are quite different ways of looking at it, do you still want to say that the chessboard is absolutely 'composite'? (PI 47a, d)

Now these examples show only that we lack a clear conception of *what components* a complex object has. This is not to show that we have no absolute concept of simplicity or compositeness at all. The Wittgenstein of the *Tractatus* might reply that the existence of more than one possible decomposition of the chessboard shows only that we can take various *routes* to the final analysis, just as somebody who thought that words were ultimately composites of letters could still admit that there is nothing to choose between saying (a) that 'logic' is composed of 'lo' and 'gic' and (b) that it is composed of 'log' and 'ic'.

But it *is* appropriate for Wittgenstein to complain against his earlier self that the *Tractatus* does nothing to *explain* an absolute notion of simplicity to somebody who does not already possess one. Now you might propose that we treat the Tractarian *motivation* for simplicity as definitive of it. More precisely: the reason for thinking that there are simples in the first place is that the universe must be composed of *indestructible*, that is, *necessarily existent* items. So could we perhaps take 'simple' in the *Tractatus* system to *mean* 'indestructible'?

Doing so would make it clear enough what 'simple' means; but it would still leave it quite unclear whether or not anything *is* simple. It is hard to see how a *particular* could be indestructible: it appears straightforward enough to imagine the non-existence of *any* particular and so there must be a presumption against its necessary existence. What about universals?

> "Something red can be destroyed [says the interlocutor], but red cannot be destroyed, and that is why the meaning of the word 'red' is independent of the existence of a red thing." – Certainly it makes no sense to say that the colour red is torn up or pounded to bits. But don't we say "The red is vanishing"? And don't clutch at the idea of our always being able to bring red before our mind's eye even when there is nothing red any more. That is just as if you choose to say that there would still always be a chemical reaction producing a red flame. – For suppose you cannot remember the colour any more? (PI 57)

It is not clear what it *means* to say that red exists if it doesn't mean that *something* red exists. In what sense, then, can universals be called indestructible?

But then what was wrong with the train of thought that took us to the allied notions of simplicity and indestructibility in the first place? Recall what it was: in order for our thoughts to be true or false in all possibilities, there must be something in each of those possibilities for those thoughts to be *about*. Wittgenstein discusses this line of thought in the following passage:

> "What the names in language signify [says the interlocutor] must be indestructible; for it must be possible to describe the state of affairs in which everything destructible is destroyed. And this description will contain words; and what corresponds to these cannot then be destroyed, for otherwise the words would have no meaning." I must not saw off the branch on which I am sitting.
>
> One might, of course, object at once that this description would have to except itself from the destruction. (PI 55)

This immediate objection encapsulates a serious problem with the original train of thought. It was being supposed that in order for an *actual* thought or description meaningfully to say something about a counterfactual situation, there must be something in the *counterfactual* situation to make the thought or description meaningful. But that is simply false. When *we* assess a description with respect to a non-actual situation we require only that the description *is* meaningful; we do *not* require that the description *would have been* meaningful if that non-actual situation *had* obtained, as follows from the fact (to which Wittgenstein is ironically alluding) that we can certainly describe possible situations in which the description would not even have *existed*.

There is another way of being tempted into thinking that the preconditions of language are in some sense necessary. Suppose that it is necessary for certain coloured things to exist in order that certain colour-*words* have a meaning. Suppose in particular that the word 'sepia' depends for its meaning upon the existence of a certain unreproducible standard sample of that colour, with which we compare candidates for that predicate; this may be because to the unaided eye sepia objects are chromatically indistinguishable from objects of other shades. Then in one sense the sentence 'There is a sepia sample' *cannot* be false: for if it were false, then the expression 'sepia' occurring within it would have no meaning; and so that 'sentence' would be not false after all but meaningless. And similarly one might think that the objects that our language depends upon for its meaning are indestructible, simply because a sentence asserting the *non-existence* of any of them would be meaningless if true.

But of course to say that 'There is a sepia sample' is *true if meaningful* is not to say that the sepia sample *itself* exists necessarily. It is only to say something about the presuppositions of the language in which it is stated:

> We can put it like this: This sample is an instrument of the language used in ascriptions of colour. In this language-game it is not something that is represented, but is a means of representation . . . What looks as if it *had* to exist, is part of the language. It is a paradigm in our language-game; something with which comparison is made. And this may be an important observation; but it is none the less an observation concerning our language-game – our method of representation. (PI 50)

Much the same could be said about the objects of the *Tractatus*.

1.3.4. Analysis

At PI 60–4 Wittgenstein argues as follows: first that it is unclear whether the analysis envisaged in the *Tractatus* really yields something with the *same* meaning as what it operates upon; and second that in any case it does not reveal that meaning more *perspicuously*.

In connection with the first point he starts by simply *denying* that analysis reveals more clearly the thought that you had all along and which you originally expressed by the unanalysed sentence.

> When I say: "My broom is in the corner", – is this really a statement about the broomstick and the brush? Well, it could at any rate be replaced by a statement giving the position of the stick and the position of the brush . . . Then does someone who says that the broom is in the corner really mean: the broomstick is there, and so is the brush, and the broomstick is fixed in the brush? – If we were to ask anyone if he meant this he would probably say that he had not thought specially of the broomstick or specially of the brush at all. And that

would be the *right* answer, for he meant to speak neither of the stick nor of the brush in particular. (PI 60)

As it stands this answer invites the reply that even if you didn't 'think specially' of the brush or of the broomstick, still they *were* in some sense latent in what you meant all along. Compare: if I give somebody the order to count to 1,000, it is likely that I won't 'think specially' of the step from 625 to 626; and yet if he goes straight from 625 to 627 it would be right for me to say that he had deviated from what I had *all along meant* him to do (cf. PI 187). We shall return to this point (see 3.3).

In any case Wittgenstein continues with a discussion of the *order* 'Bring me the broom'. He introduces letters (a) and (b) to denote language-games in which (a) whole instruments – for example, brooms – or (b) their parts – for example, brushes – are given names for use in orders. Thus (a) might contain the order 'Bring me the broom'; (b) might contain the order 'Bring me the broomstick and the brush which is fitted onto it.' Now, must the 'analysed' order in (b) have the same meaning as the 'unanalysed' order in (a)? Wittgenstein invites us to imagine a case where it is not so clear:

> Suppose for instance that the person who is given the orders in (a) and (b) has to look up a table co-ordinating names and pictures before bringing what is required. Does he do *the same* when he carries out an order in (a) and the corresponding one in (b)? – Yes and no. (PI 62)

Presumably yes because he brings the same object in both cases; presumably no because this action has a different *precedent* in each case.

The relevance of this point – whether he *does* the same – to the one at issue – whether the orders *mean* the same – relies upon an extension of the equation at PI 43 between meaning and *use* (discussed at 1.2). There he had said that in a large range of cases the meaning of a word is its use in the language; he now implicitly supposes that the meaning of a *sentence* too is its use in the language, where the 'use' of an order covers things like: what somebody does when he obeys it.

Now a defender of the *Tractatus* needn't grant this assumption or at any rate its applicability to the question of analysis.

He might maintain that orders, questions and descriptions, were never the intended subjects of Tractarian analysis. The intended subjects of analysis are instead the *senses* that are common to all of them. For instance, if we take the description 'Caesar crossed the Rubicon.' and the question 'Did Caesar cross the Rubicon?', it is plausible that they each have something in common as well as something not in common. What they have in common is their sense: the 'assumption' (PI 22) or truth-condition, *Caesar's crossing the Rubicon*; and what they do not have in common is that the question is *asking whether* the truth-condition obtains whereas the description is *saying that* it does. By similar reasoning we could make a case that an order shares something with both a question and a description: 'Shut the door!' shares with 'Is the door shut?' and 'The door is shut.' – what might be called the obedience-condition of the first sentence, the affirmation-condition of the second and the truth-condition of the third.

And – the defender of the *Tractatus* will continue – what concerned me all along was how thoughts could be about possible situations in which there seemed to *be* nothing for them to be about. And this question arises for questions and orders as much as for descriptions. But if we say that the thought that Napoleon conquered Russia in 1812 is really about indestructible objects, then both the question 'Did Napoleon conquer Russia in 1812?' and the description 'Napoleon conquered Russia in 1812.' must be about the same indestructible objects, because one of them is asking just what the other is asserting. So what I was really trying to analyse all along was the *sense* of our thoughts.

And it follows – he will conclude – that you cannot criticize me on the grounds that an analysed *order* has a different *use* from its unanalysed version. For this does not show that the analysed *sense* is different from the unanalysed one. The only thing that could show a difference in the *sense* of the two analysed and unanalysed orders would be a difference in the obedience-conditions of the order in (a) and the order in (b). But as we can see, these are perfectly alike: to bring someone the broom *is* to bring him the broomstick fixed in the brush.

There is a brief and unsatisfactory response to this at PI 22, where Wittgenstein rejects the idea 'that every assertion contains an assumption, which is the thing that is asserted'. He objects that the idea arises from the possibility of separating the assumption from the rest of the assertion, so that instead of 'Caesar crossed the Rubicon' one might write 'It is asserted: that Caesar crossed the Rubicon', where 'that Caesar crossed the Rubicon' is the assumption or sense of the assertion. But, he continues, if this possibility of rewriting *is* the basis of that idea it is a bad one:

> We might very well also write every statement in the form of a question followed by a "Yes"; for instance: "Is it raining? Yes!" Would this shew that every statement contained a question?

Of course the answer is no.

But then this 'possibility of rewriting' need *not* have been the motivation for the idea in the first place. Isn't it rather that the separation of the sense of a sentence from the other factors that generate its use is an obvious prerequisite for obtaining a systematic explanation of that use? It is part of my knowing how to speak and write English that I know how to use both the description 'Caesar crossed the Rubicon' and the question 'Did Caesar cross the Rubicon?' Isn't it likely or at least a good working supposition that the best explanation of these two abilities will appeal to something that they have in common – namely, my knowledge of their *sense*? As we shall soon discuss Wittgenstein didn't think that philosophy should try to explain anything (see 2.3); but apart from this quite generally applicable stance it is hard to see what motivates his opposition to the *Tractatus* on this fundamental point.

The other line of objection to analysis appears at PI 63–4, where he raises the question of whether something essential to the thought might not be lost by the very process of isolating its constituents ('We murder to dissect'). He gives the example of people who have names not for coloured shapes (as at PI 48) but for certain *combinations* of them, so that, for instance, a rectangle which is half red and half green (i.e. a red square to the left of a green one) is called 'U' and one that is half green, half white is called 'V'. And he compares this language-game with another (i.e. that at PI 48) into which, for example, 'U' would get translated as 'RG', where 'R' denotes red squares and 'G' denotes green ones.

Presumably what has been lost in translation is the *unity* for its speakers of the experience that their language described using the *single* expressions 'U' and 'V'. For there is a difference between the bare experience of seeing a red square adjacent to a green square and the gestalt experience of seeing a 'red-and-green' rectangle. And the proposed translation of 'U' as 'RG' effaces this difference. *We* have similar experiences too: 'Think of the cases where we say "This arrangement of colours (say the French tricolor) has a quite special character"' (PI 64). Or again, when we hear music we often hear a chord as a *unity* of different notes: it is not at all the same thing as merely hearing one thing *at the same time* as another, as happens when, for example, one hears somebody's mobile phone go off in the middle of a concert. But why could not the analysis also capture this unity? For instance, why could one not analyse the gestalt experience recorded by 'U' as, say, 'R*G'? – Here the sign '*' is a conventional indication of the unity of what we may still regard as the phenomenological elements of the experience.

In the face of that objection another of Wittgenstein's examples would seem more to the point:

> I could imagine someone saying that he saw a red and yellow star, but did not see anything yellow – because he sees a star as, so to speak, a *conjunction* of coloured parts which he cannot separate. (RFM VII-65)

So an analysis of a 'red-and-yellow star' experience (see the illustration in RFM) might get rendered in his language as TS, where 'S' denotes a star-shape and T denotes the composite 'red-and-yellow' chromatic experience. It would now seem to *falsify* his experience to translate its description as 'RYS' or even 'R*YS' for that makes it seem as though yellow was *already* part of the experience; but the fact that he might notice the yellow on closer inspection clearly needn't mean that it was part of his experience all along (cf. PI 171b). But the author of the *Tractatus* might reply that that only shows that analysis can reveal unnoticed features of the thought – and we have already seen (in connection with the 'broom' example) how he might further defend *that*.

Finally, it is worth mentioning that in his pre-*Tractatus Note-books* Wittgenstein toyed with a conception of analysis that gave much greater weight to the concerns raised at PI 63–4 than is evident from the finished work. He wrote on 18 June 1915:

> It seems to me perfectly possible that patches in our visual field are simple objects, in that we do not perceive any single point of a patch separately; the visual appearances of stars even seem certainly to be so. What I mean is: if, e.g., I say that this watch is not in the drawer, there is absolutely no need for it to FOLLOW LOGICALLY that a wheel that is in the watch is not in the drawer, for perhaps I had not the least knowledge that the wheel was in the watch, and hence could not have meant by 'this watch' the complex in which the wheel occurs. And it is certain – moreover – that I do not see all the parts of my theoretical visual field. Who knows whether I see infinitely many points? (NB 64–5)

The entries from around this period offer a quite different vision of the 'simple objects' lying at the limits of analysis than what you would gather from the *Tractatus* itself. According to the for-mer, what distinguishes terms for simple from terms for complex objects is the *role of those terms within the language*, not the metaphysical complexity or compositeness of what they denote, just as PI 50 proposes. So that if, for example, the complexity of Socrates is irrelevant to our use of 'Socrates' in the language (e.g. in inferences involving 'Socrates'), the term 'Socrates' may be said to denote a simple in that language; and if we replaced it with an 'analysis' – say, 'The composite object consisting of Socrates's head stuck on to Socrates's body' – we should *no lon-ger be speaking the same language*, just as PI 64b proposes. It is striking that Wittgenstein's criticisms of the *Tractatus* concep-tions of simplicity and analysis appear to be recommending, or at least to be allowing for, a reversion to ones that he had enter-tained so far beforehand.[6]

1.4. 'Sentences are combinations of names'

The final element of the Augustinian picture that I discuss here is the idea that sentences are combinations of other expressions. It is not explicit in the quotation from the *Confessions* at PI 1 but it *is* present in Wittgenstein's gloss upon it:

> These words, it seems to me, give us a particular picture of the essence of human language. It is this: the individual words in language name objects – sentences are combinations of such names. (PI 1)

We have already seen reason to doubt that all words are *names* in any of three senses; so we have reason to doubt that all sentences are combinations of *names*. But can we say that in general they are *combinations* at all, that is, of *any* sorts of word? As with referentialism we shall consider first the application of that idea to everyday language, and then to the thoughts behind it, of which Tractarian analysis was supposed to reveal the structure.

It is clear enough that many everyday sentences are not combinations of expressions at all but rather consist of a *single* word. This is indeed quite obviously true of *all* sentences of the imaginary language at PI 2 (here conceived as a complete language): its only sentences are 'Beam!', 'Slab!', and the like. And while plenty of English sentences *are* combinations, plenty of them are not. 'Think of exclamations alone . . . Water! Away! Ow! Help! Fine! No!' (PI 27).

But then what about the thoughts that these sentences express – are *they* essentially composite? In the *Tractatus* he had thought so: according to it a thought is a proposition with a sense (TLP 4); but a proposition can only *have* a sense by picturing a possible situation (TLP 3), and:

> It is only in so far as a proposition is logically segmented that it is a picture of a situation.
> (Even the proposition, *Ambulo*, is composite: for its stem with a different ending yields a different sense, and so does its ending with a different stem.) (TLP 4.032)

We can take two further points away from this section. What we can gather from his comment on *Ambulo* is that what it *is* for a proposition to be composite, to be a combination of other expressions, is for it to have something of semantic significance in common with *other* propositions – indeed Wittgenstein goes so far as to present each 'component' of a proposition *as* the set

of propositions that 'contain' it (TLP 3.31–3.318; cf. TLP 5.5261b).
And what we can take away from TLP 4.032a in conjunction
with the picture theory is that this kind of composition is a
necessary condition on meaningfulness.

But then what about the language of PI 2? None of *its*
sentences appear to have anything of semantic significance in
common with any other sentences of it, for example, 'Beam!'
and 'Slab!' have no such thing in common.[7] From the perspective
of the *Tractatus* this would have to be one of those cases in
which the structure of everyday language conceals the structure
of the thoughts that it is supposed to be expressing (TLP 4.002d).
According to it the sentences 'Beam!' and 'Slab!' would have to
be expressing thoughts that did have a common element, for
example, *I want you to bring me a beam*; and *I want you to bring
me a slab*.

Wittgenstein's discussion of these matters at PI 19–21 covers
both points. On the first point he is in partial agreement with
his earlier self. He agrees that meaning a sentence as composite
or simple is not so to speak a local property of the utterance
but rather to do with the language in which it belongs. You
cannot tell whether, for example, the utterance 'Bring me a slab'
is meant as one *long* word or as four *short* ones by attending
solely to *it*; instead you must look at the *other* expressive resources
of English.

> I think we shall be inclined to say: we mean the sentence as
> *four* words when we use it in contrast with other sentences such
> as "*Hand* me a slab", "Bring *him* a slab", "Bring *two* slabs",
> etc.; that is, in contrast with sentences containing the separate
> words of our command in other combinations. (PI 20)

But note that this agreement is not over the compositeness or
otherwise of its *meaning* but only over whether the *sentence* 'Bring
me a slab' is meant as composite or simple or as a single word.
What Wittgenstein says here could equally be applied as a criterion
for whether or not, for example, an intrinsically meaningless
pattern of sound in a composition is a chord or a single note – we
may settle it by asking whether its elements recur in other combinations in other music of its genre. He is not giving a criterion
for whether the *thought* behind the sentence 'Bring me a slab', or

that behind the sentence 'Slab!' in the language of PI 2, is *itself* composite or simple. So he is not here agreeing with the *Tractatus* line that these thoughts must themselves be composite.

It is worth noting that in the course of expounding this view of the compositeness of sentences he attacks a faulty understanding of it, one of which the *Tractatus* is entirely innocent but which is still of interest because of its analogy with other views that *do* appear in the earlier work. The view that I have in mind is the idea that using the (composite) sentence 'in contrast with others' is a matter of accompanying one's overt utterance with some unobservable mental process. Wittgenstein effectively criticizes that idea by trying to get more definite about it; for as soon as one tries to be specific about what this accompaniment is supposed to be one finds oneself describing something that plainly does *not* happen:

> But what does using one sentence in contrast with others consist in? Do the others, perhaps, hover before one's mind? *All* of them? And *while* one is saying the one sentence, or before, or afterwards? – No. Even if such an explanation rather tempts us, we need only think for a moment of what actually happens in order to see that we are going astray here. (PI 20)

To say that you mean a sentence as composite is *not* to describe an inner process that accompanies the utterance; rather it is a comparison of that sentence with others that occur in the language that you then used. The mistake that Wittgenstein here criticizes does not occur in the *Tractatus*; but other variations upon its ground bass do occur there. That ground bass is the idea that meaning, understanding, intending, attending and thinking, and so on are inner processes that go on *alongside* their verbal expressions. Wittgenstein's criticisms of *this* idea's various realizations runs through *Philosophical Investigations* like a scarlet thread.

And one realization of it that *does* occur in the *Tractatus* is that way of understanding 4.032a that makes it compatible with the language of the builders at PI 2. Remember that speakers of that language cannot have meant the sentence 'Slab!' as composite, at least not by the criterion that we have just seen proposed at PI 20; for it has nothing in common with 'Beam!' or any other sentence in the language. But according to the *Tractatus* builder

A nonetheless *means* something complex when she says 'Slab!'
That is to say, perspicuous representations of what she meant by
'Slab!' and 'Beam!' would between them show a common element,
for example, what 'I want you to bring me a slab' shares with
'I want you to bring me a beam'.

> But how do you do this: how do you *mean that* while you *say*
> "Slab!"? Do you say the unshortened sentence to yourself?
> And why should I translate the call "Slab!" into a different
> expression in order to say what someone means by it? And if
> they mean the same thing – why should I not say: "When he
> says 'Slab!' he means 'Slab!'"? . . . – – But when I call "Slab!",
> then what I want is, *that he should bring me a slab*! – – Certainly,
> but does 'wanting this' consist in thinking in some form or
> other a different sentence from the one you utter? (PI 19)

The error is different from the one that PI 20 attacks but the
form of the criticism is the same: if we look at what actually
goes on, we are *not* aware of any composite act of meaning
that accompanies the utterance of a one-word sentence. Why
say then that you really mean something composite?

Well, one reason might be a desire to explain what the
Tractatus emphasizes at 4.02–4.027: the fact that a proposition
can communicate something *new*. More specifically, how can
we explain the fact that the capacity to understand certain
propositions brings in its wake the capacity to understand a
whole range of others, unless we suppose that understanding
a proposition means grasping something *composite* and hence
also grasping what arrangements of its elements can express?

We can illustrate this point with a slight elaboration upon the
builders' language of PI 2. Suppose that in this new language
A calls out 'Slab!' (or 'Beam!' or . . .) in a *low*-pitched voice
when she wants B to bring her a *slab*; and she calls out 'Slab!' in
a *high*-pitched voice when she wants B to bring her *anything
but* a slab. Let us write 'Slab +' for the first, low-pitched, type
of utterance, and 'Slab –' for the second, high-pitched, type of
utterance. Now in accordance with the way that *Philosophical
Investigations* presents it, we may say that for the builder's
assistant to understand the order is for her to respond to it in

the right way. So it is logically possible for somebody to understand, say, 'Slab –' but not 'Slab +', or to understand *both* such
orders but *not* to understand *either* 'Beam –' *or* 'Beam +'. And
such understanding could be imparted by explicit training in the
use of (i.e. in the correct response to) an expression, or it could
be left to the builder's assistant to pick it up by watching others.

Now suppose we discover that whenever a builder's assistant
has achieved by any means an understanding of the orders
'Beam +' and 'Slab –', she has also and without any further
instruction come to grasp the orders 'Beam –' and 'Slab +'. This
phenomenon would cry out for explanation: it is a very simple
instance of 'the fact that we can understand the sense of a
propositional sign without its sense having been explained to us'
(TLP 4.02). And isn't the most obvious explanation just this:
that the builder's assistant has a *separate* grasp of (a) the *words*
'Beam' and 'Slab' and (b) their pitch; and it is through a *recomb-
ination* of these principles that her grasp of both 'Beam +' and
'Slab –' gives rise to a grasp of 'Beam –' and 'Slab +'?

In that case we should have a *reason* for appealing to a certain
complexity in her thoughts to explain certain regularities in her
behaviour. Such complexity need not be that of any conscious or
introspectible process of the sort that PI 19 and PI 20 attack;
rather, the notion of thought that we need is a *theoretical* one
that we accept only because of the behavioural data that it
explains. I am not saying that that is how it is with human beings;
but I *am* saying that it is an empirical question whether it is so,
and that there is at least *prima facie* reason to think that it is so
for languages that go beyond that of PI 2 to the extent and in the
direction that my elaboration of it has indicated.

Let me conclude this section by remarking upon a theme that
connects it with the ones on ostension and functional unity: the
idea that certain mental or intentional occurrences are or involve
inner processes accompanying their visible or audible expression. So far we have seen four phenomena to which it has initially
attractive application: (a) the meaningful use of linguistic expressions (1.1); (b) attending to the colour of something (rather than,
for example, its shape) (1.2); (c) meaning a sentence as composite rather than simple (1.4); (d) meaning something composite
when uttering a simple sentence (1.4).Wittgenstein diagnoses

one *source* of this attraction in the following summing-up of his discussion of ostension:

> And we do here what we do in a host of similar cases: because we cannot specify any *one* bodily action which we call pointing to the shape (as opposed, for example, to the colour), we say that a *spiritual* [*geistige*: mental, intellectual] activity corresponds to these words.
>
> Where our language suggests a body and there is none: there, we should like to say, is a *spirit*. (PI 36)

A proper understanding of this remark requires some understanding of his doctrine of *family resemblance* – to which we now turn.

SECTION 2. FAMILY RESEMBLANCE AND THE IDEAL OF PRECISION

2.1. Family resemblance

Recall our discussion of PI 60–4 (1.3.4). There Wittgenstein had tried to raise doubts about the identity of two pairs of language-games, or two ways of playing each of two language-games. The first pair consisted of (a) an 'unanalysed' and (b) an 'analysed' language of orders in which one had to obey an order by correlating names with pictures (PI 62). The second pair consisted of (c) an 'analysed' language-game of the sort described at PI 48, that is, one in which we concatenate letters such as 'R' and 'G' to describe the coloured squares that we see before us; and (d) an 'unanalysed' language-game in which atomic expressions like 'U' and 'V' are used to characterize apparently composite pairs of squares, for example, 'U' signifies a red square adjacent to a green one. The intuitive or at least Tractarian idea was that the very *same* meanings that get expressed in (a) and (d) also get more perspicuous expression in (b) and (c). And we have seen Wittgenstein's reasons in PI for wanting to deny this.

We have also glanced at his reason in the *Tractatus* for wishing quite firmly to maintain it. That reason was basically a certain conception of the essence of language (i.e. its propositions). The essence of a proposition is that it describes how things stand.

> It now seems possible to give the most general propositional form: that is, to give a description of the propositions of *any* sign-language *whatsoever* in such a way that every possible

sense can be expressed by a symbol satisfying the description, and every symbol satisfying the description can express a sense, provided that the meanings of the names are suitably chosen.

It is clear that *only* what is essential to the most general propositional form may be included in its description – for otherwise it would not be the most general form . . .

The general form of a proposition is: This is how things stand. (TLP 4.5)

Now to say that things stand in a certain way is to pick out a possible way in which things *can* stand; so two propositions say the same thing if they pick out the same possible ways in which things can stand. That is: we can identify the meanings of propositions p and q just in case they would be *true* in just the same circumstances and *false* in just the same circumstances (this follows from TLP 4.4). And we can extend the account straightforwardly to orders as already sketched (1.3.4): orders O1 and O2 express the same sense just in case they would be *obeyed* in the same circumstances and *disobeyed* in the same circumstances. And from this account of the essence of language there follows a straightforward verdict on the cases (a)–(d). An order in (a) has the same meaning as the corresponding one in (b) because they have the same *obedience*-conditions; and the description 'U' in (d) has the same meaning as 'RG' in (c) because they have the same *truth*-conditions.

With this in mind we can ask whether *Philosophical Investigations* offers any *rival* account of the essence of language that justifies its alternative verdict on cases (a)–(d). Wittgenstein puts the demand for such an account into the mouth of an imaginary accuser:

You take the easy way out! You talk about all sorts of language-games, but have nowhere said what the essence of a language-game, and hence of language, is: what is common to all these activities, and what makes them into language or parts of language. So you let yourself off the very part of the investigation that once gave you yourself most headache, the part about the *general form of propositions* and of language. (PI 65)

At PI 65b Wittgenstein admits the justice of this comment, and this opens a sequence in which he elaborates upon why, contrary to what he thought in the *Tractatus*, no such account is possible.

For it seems as though an account of the necessary and sufficient conditions of language *must* be possible; otherwise, what explanation is there for our applying of the word 'language' in just the cases where we *do* apply it? This question, which hovers in the background of the discussion around PI 65, plays upon a very important theme. It is the idea that to understand an expression is to be in some mental state, or to have some mental item within one's purview, that *guides* one's use of that expression. Wittgenstein is going to argue from a number of directions that things are more complicated than that. For first, there need not *be* any such inner guide to one's use of an expression; and second, even in cases where there is, there are still many different ways in which it can be said to *guide* one's use. I shall return to this second point (3.1.1) but let us now consider an instance of the first that has immediate bearing.

What Wittgenstein argues is that it need not be the case that we apply a word in all cases because of one necessary and sufficient condition that those cases have in common. To establish this he considers the word 'game':

> Consider for example the proceedings that we call "games". I mean board-games, card-games, ball-games, Olympic games, and so on. What is common to them all? – Don't say: "There *must* be something common, or they would not be called 'games'" – but *look and see* whether there is anything common to all. – For if you look at them you will not see something that is common to *all*, but similarities, relationships, and a whole series of them at that. To repeat: don't think, but look! – Look for example at board-games, with their multifarious relationships. Now pass to card-games; here you find many correspondences with the first group, but many common features drop out, and others appear. When we pass next to ball-games much that is common is retained, but much is lost. – Are they all 'amusing'? Compare chess with noughts and crosses. (Etc. PI 66)

The example is compelling; and even if by some feat of ingenuity someone managed to find a non-trivial necessary and sufficient condition for being a game, it would still be clear that *that* was not why we applied the word 'game' in all the cases where we do apply it. Rather the explanation that Wittgenstein appears here to be gesturing at is this: the reason we apply the expression 'game' to certain activities is because of their bearing a similarity – or perhaps some other relationship – to other things that we *already* call 'games'. And one might give more or less similar explanations for the use of many words.[8] Wittgenstein calls these relationships *family resemblances* and writes that the items falling under them *form a family* (PI 67a); I shall also say that concepts that resemble 'game' in this respect are *family resemblance concepts*.

But if I don't know the necessary and sufficient conditions for something's being a game then how am I supposed to explain to someone *else* what a game is? – Say, a child who has heard his brother say 'Let's play a game' and who wants to know what 'game' means; or to a native Francophone who knows enough English to understand an explanation of that word but not yet the word itself? Well, what do we actually *do* in these cases? – we give the pupil *examples* of games and we say: 'This *and similar things* are called "games"' (PI 69). And the vagueness inherent in the word 'similar' is not a vague way of gesturing at something that I know more precisely but for some reason cannot say (PI 71b): for there is nothing more *to* know about what 'game' means. And if the explanation works, so that my pupil now uses the word 'game' as I do (allowing for independent differences of opinion between us), why should we not say that I have told him *precisely* what I meant by it?[9] I shall return to the issue of vagueness at 2.2.

Now as well as to 'game' Wittgenstein applies this point to 'language', 'language-game' and 'proposition': there need be no one thing that all languages or propositions have in common, for there need be no one such thing that explains our pattern of applying these words. 'We see that what we call "sentence" and "language" has not the formal unity that I imagined [in the *Tractatus*], but is the family of structures more or less related to one another' (PI 108).

But just how telling is this point against the *Tractatus*? Suppose that Wittgenstein's earlier self agreed that our ordinary use of the word 'language', like our ordinary use of, say, 'matter', is something of a mess. He might still insist that what he was discussing in the *Tractatus* was not the 'language' of everyday speech – quite possibly no one thing answers to *that* – but to a somewhat more regimented *successor*-concept that picks out a particular *kind* of language-game of the utmost importance: the language-game of describing how things actually stand. One can certainly agree with *Philosophical Investigations* that it is not essential to *all* language-games that they describe how things stand in some respect (cf. PI 363); but why should it not be essential to a very important and interesting subset of them: a subset moreover that includes the language of science? And if we do restrict ourselves to that subset, why can we not say that on the criteria that are appropriate *for them*, the very meanings that sentences of the language-games (a) and (d) express obscurely get clear expression in the language-games (b) and (c) respectively? But this was the question that prompted Wittgenstein's discussion of family resemblance in the first place. So it looks as though we might accept the main conclusions of that discussion while also holding on to the Tractarian ideas that they were supposed to dislodge.

Of course this is not to say that the *Tractatus* has given a correct account of how even some limited sector of language achieves what it seems to. Indeed there are still many serious criticisms of its detail to come. But it *is* to say that considerations of family resemblance do not undermine the *Tractatus* project itself; they only restrict its scope.

I return finally to the point that concluded chapter 1. Recall Wittgenstein's denial at PI 34 that what distinguishes the act of attending to something's shape from, for example, attending to its colour – say, in the course of giving an ostensive definition – is some accompanying experience. His criticism, which seemed decisive, was that even if such an experience took place in him, somebody who went on in consequence to use the defined term as a *colour* term would have been attending all along to the colour and not to the shape. This point is so straightforward and compelling that it raises the question of how things could even have *seemed* otherwise. Why was the idea of an accompanying experience even *prima facie* attractive?

At PI 36 Wittgenstein says that 'we do here what we do in a host of similar cases: because we cannot specify any *one* bodily action which we call pointing to the shape . . . we say that a *spiritual* activity corresponds to these words.' PI 33 has already empha- sized the fact that we cannot find 'any *one* bodily action' (recall the list of ways in which one can attend to the colour blue, PI 33); but the reason that this makes us postulate a single type of spiritual activity *behind* all of these behavioural ones is precisely because we think that they *must* all have one thing in common. But now we see that they need not: 'attending to the shape' might be a family resemblance concept. That is to say, it might correctly describe *different* bodily actions on different occasions; but it does not owe this to any one spiritual action that unites all such cases.

We have already seen four cases of temptation to postulate a spiritual activity behind the bodily ones that seem to express it. These were (a) the meaningful use of linguistic expressions; (b) attending to the colour of something (rather than, for example, its shape); (c) meaning a sentence as composite rather than simple; (d) meaning something composite when uttering a simple sentence. And we have seen how consideration of family resemblance explains the temptation in case (b) – or rather how our *failure* to consider it does.

It is not so clear that such a failure is what explains the temptation in case (d): what lay behind that was rather the *Tractatus* demand for compositeness as a necessary condition upon meaningfulness. But in cases (a) and (c) the explanation *is* plausible. Case (a) was the temptation to say, of the grocer of PI 1, that his overt use of 'apple' was the tip of an iceberg: behind all of its various uses is an act of mental comparison that explains it (e.g. comparison with an idea). And one reason for thinking this is the fear that otherwise there would be no *one* explanation for all of his various uses of the word 'apple'. But why *should* there be just one? And in case (c) we suffer from *two* illusions: first we think that 'meaning it as composite' must be something that goes on *when* he says it (here it is occurrences of 'meaning it' as gerund or gerundive that fool us); and then finding no one 'bodily action' that goes on when you mean a sentence as, for example, four words rather than one. The second illusion arises from a failure to see that instances of 'meaning it as composite' might form a family.

2.2. Vagueness

2.2.1. *Vagueness and family resemblance*

We can best introduce Wittgenstein's notion of vagueness by means of a passage in which he appears to confuse it with family resemblance:

> How should we explain to someone what a game is? I imagine
> that we should describe *games* to him, and we might add:
> "This *and similar things* are called 'games'". And do we know
> any more about it ourselves? Is it only other people whom we
> cannot tell exactly what a game is? – But this is not ignorance.
> We do not know the boundaries because none have been
> drawn. To repeat, we can draw a boundary – for a special
> purpose. Does it take that to make the concept usable? Not at
> all! (Except for that special purpose.) (PI 69)

A vague concept is one whose application is not *everywhere*
determined by one's grasp of it: thus, for example, the concept
'blue' is vague because, although somebody who grasps it will
typically know that the sky is blue and that grass is not, there
may well be objects that he will not classify in either category
even though he knows everything relevant to settling it (i.e. he
is looking at them in good light, his eyes are functioning well,
etc.). We may call objects of this latter sort 'borderline cases';
so the existence or at least possibility of borderline cases can be
taken as the defining feature of vague concepts. In this passage
Wittgenstein appears to be suggesting that 'game' is vague. ('We
do not know the boundaries because none have been drawn.')

But we should distinguish family resemblance from vagueness. Family resemblance is neither necessary nor sufficient for
vagueness. Not sufficient because a concept might have a family
resemblance character and yet not admit of borderline cases.
Thus take Wittgenstein's own example of number:

> And for instance the kinds of number form a family in the
> same way [as do games]. Why do we call something a "num-
> ber"? Well, perhaps because it has a – direct – relationship
> with several things that have hitherto been called number;
> and this may be said to give it an indirect relationship to other
> things that we call the same name. (PI 67)

In fact these relationships appear to be quite different. Thus
integers count as numbers because they are what you get if you
close the set of natural numbers under subtraction; rational

numbers count as numbers because they are what you get if you close the set of integers under division (except by zero); real numbers count as numbers because they are what you get if you close the set of rational numbers under the operation that forms suprema from arbitrary sets of them that are bounded above; and complex numbers are numbers because they are what you get if you close the set of real numbers under the operation that forms roots of arbitrary polynomials with real coefficients. But each of these relationships has a perfectly *definite* extension – there are no 'borderline numbers' in that sense in which there might be borderline blue objects. So the concept of number is not a vague concept.[10]

Or again, one might imagine that the concept of 'game' was circumscribed in such a way that there could not be any 'borderline games'; and yet in such a way that it still included board-games, card-games, Olympic games and the rest. In that case it would be *true* to say that games form a family but false to say that 'no boundaries have been drawn'. And although this is not how things actually are, its *possibility* suffices to establish what the actual situation with numbers also shows: that family resemblance does not suffice for vagueness.

Nor does vagueness suffice for family resemblance. The concept of a 'tricolor' admits of straightforward analysis: it applies (let us say) to flags that carry a certain arrangement of a red, a white and a blue vertical stripe. And it is *because* we deem them to have that arrangement that we apply it to just the flags that we do. So 'tricolor' is not a family resemblance concept. On the other hand it *is* a vague one since 'red stripe' and 'blue stripe' clearly admit of borderline cases: if any concepts are vague then they are. Hence so too is the concept that is compounded from them in the way that 'tricolor' is: it is easy to imagine a borderline tricolor. So a concept can be vague without being a family resemblance concept; and a concept can be a family resemblance concept without being vague.

2.2.2. *Vagueness and analysis*
But vagueness is as relevant as family resemblance to the discussion at this point, though for a slightly different reason. The discussion at PI 60–4 concerned the language-games (a)–(d) (defined at the start of this chapter). The whole issue between

Wittgenstein and his interlocutor concerned the identities of these language-games. More precisely, it was over whether the differences between the *uses* of sentences in (a) ('Bring me the broom') and (b) ('Bring me the broomstick which is fitted in the brush') constituted a difference in their meanings; and equally over whether the differences between the uses of sentences in (c) ('RG') and (d) ('U') constituted a difference in *their* meanings. And we may try to settle this issue in the manner of the *Tractatus*: find the essence of language and propositions and then apply it to the present case. We have seen that Wittgenstein rejects that because he thinks that language-games form a family.

But the aim of comparing language-games (c) and (d) had been to illustrate a particular sort of point about analysis:

> To say . . . that a sentence in (b) is an 'analysed' form of one in (a) readily seduces us into thinking that that the former is the more fundamental form; that it alone shews what is meant by the other, and so on. For example, we think: If you have only the unanalysed form you miss the analysis; but if you know the analysed form that gives you everything. – But may I not say that an aspect of the former is lost upon you in the *latter* case as well as the former? (PI 63)

The point about (c) and (d) was that something of the gestalt aspect of the experiences recorded in the unanalysed (d) ('U') is lost in translation to the analysed (c) ('RG'). But there is another way to illustrate the point at PI 63, for another aspect that may also be lost in analysis is the essential vagueness of the unanalysed expressions; that this is so is one of the things that Wittgenstein's discussion of vagueness aims to establish.

In the *Tractatus* the process of analysis was supposed to lead to the elementary propositions out of which the analysandum was truth-functionally constructed (TLP 4.4). We might for instance analyse P ('The broom is in the corner') as O1 & O2 & O3, where O1, O2 and O3 are elementary propositions (as it might be, 'The broomstick is in the corner', 'The brush is in the corner', 'The broomstick is fixed in the brush'). The analysis is supposed to preserve truth-conditions, so P is true in just those situations in which (O1 & O2 & O3) is true, that is, in just those situations in which *each* of O1, O2 and O3 is true.

Now the elementary propositions are supposed to be maximally precise, for elementary propositions are pictures, and

> What constitutes a picture is that its elements are related to one another in a determinate way . . . The fact that the elements of a picture are related to one another in a determinate way represents that its elements are related to one another in the same way. (TLP 2.14, 2.15)

Hence every possible world is such as to make an elementary proposition definitely true or such as to make it definitely false. The same therefore applies to all truth-functional combinations of elementary propositions; and if the programme of analysis in the *Tractatus* is well-conceived then *that* means *all* propositions. So if that programme is well-conceived, *every* proposition draws a definite boundary around the possible situations that make it true: to use language is therefore also to express a thought of complete precision. 'A proposition has one and only one complete analysis. What a proposition expresses it expresses in a determinate manner' (TLP 3.25–3.251).

But Wittgenstein now argues that the vagueness of our language is essential to it. It is not that our language contains vague means of expressing precise thoughts; it is that it contains vague means of expressing *vague thoughts*. To eliminate the vagueness is to lose an aspect of what you meant all along.

At PI 70–88 he illustrates this point with various examples of vague orders, vague descriptions and vague concepts. Among these is the description 'Moses did not exist.' Wittgenstein agrees with Russell that names may be defined by means of definite descriptions, that is, expressions of the form 'The so-and-so'. Thus we might define 'Moses' by the definite description 'The man who led the Israelites through the wilderness', or by the definite description 'The man who lived at that time and place and was then called "Moses"', or by any of many other such definite descriptions (PI 79a).

Each such definition could be regarded as contributing to the analysis of 'Moses did not exist', that is, to a specification of just those possible situations in which it is true and just those in which it is false. Thus Wittgenstein's first illustrative definition would make 'Moses did not exist' true in just those situations in which no one man led the Israelites through the wilderness, even if some one man *did* do all of the *other* deeds that are commonly credited to Moses. And his second illustrative definition would make 'Moses did not exist' true just in case no one man who lived at that time and place was called 'Moses', even if someone called 'Schmoses' did *all* of the deeds that are credited to Moses (PI 79a).

But spelling out these consequences of such definitions is enough to show them up as unsatisfactory; for none of these paraphrases, nor anything as *definite* as any of them, seems to capture what I mean by 'Moses did not exist.' Wittgenstein therefore offers another definition: 'I shall perhaps say: 'By "Moses" I understand the man who did what the Bible relates of Moses, or at any rate a good deal of it" (PI 79b). So by 'Moses did not exist', according to this definition, I shall mean roughly this: 'No one man did very many of the things that the Bible relates of Moses.' *That* is a better account of what I mean.

But of course it makes my meaning vague because it gives no answer to the question '*How* many of those things?' Suppose it were discovered, for example, that there was a man whom Pharaoh's daughter rescued from the Nile, who called forth a plague of frogs upon Egypt and who was called 'Moses', but that neither he nor anyone else led the Israelites through the wilderness or brought down the Ten Commandments, and so on. Am I to say that 'Moses did not exist' is true or that it is false? Here we have a case that the definition simply does not decide, for nothing in it settles whether or not that hypothetical situation is one in which the man called 'Moses' did *very many* of the things that the Bible relates of him. So what I *meant* by 'Moses did not exist' was *not* something that drew a definite boundary around all of the possible situations that make it true. And any attempt to replace it with something that does draw such a boundary will falsify what I meant.

If someone were to draw a sharp boundary I could not acknowledge it as the one that I too always wanted to draw, or had drawn in my mind. For I did not want to draw one at all. His concept may then be said to be not the same as mine, but akin to it. The kinship is that of two pictures, one of which consists of colour patches with vague contours, and the other of patches similarly shaped and distributed, but with clear contours. (PI 76)

This beautiful metaphor is here applied to concepts but the point clearly transposes to propositions. The points on the canvas represent possible situations and the patches represent regions of points corresponding to possible situations that make a given proposition true. The point is that you can draw no sharp boundary around such regions if the proposition is 'Moses did not exist'.

2.2.3. Objections to Wittgenstein's account

But there are reasons for thinking either (a) that this must be an illusion because one *cannot* mean something vague; or (b) that illusion or not, it is pernicious because one *should* not mean something vague. The reasons that Wittgenstein discusses for (a) are as follows: (i) that if one means something vague then one doesn't really know *what* one means; (ii) that a vague concept is unusable; (iii) that the mental samples that we associate with words eliminate all vagueness in their application. For (b): that exactness is always preferable to inexactness. Let us consider these in turn.

(i) We should distinguish this objection to vagueness from a similar-sounding objection to family resemblance that we have already discussed. That other objection was that you *do* know what you mean by, for example, 'game' but for some reason you cannot *say* it. But the present objection is that you do *not* know what you mean by a vague concept. The objector says: 'If the concept "game" is uncircumscribed like that, you don't really know what you mean by "game".' Wittgenstein answers with a rhetorical question:

> When I give the description: "The ground was quite covered with plants" – do you want to say I don't know what I am talking about until I can give the definition of a plant? (PI 70)

By itself this is decisive – clearly in whatever sense of 'knowing what one is talking about' that is relevant to linguistic understanding, one *does* know what one is talking about – but it is worth saying a little more about what motivates the objection.

One way to get clearer on what somebody means in cases of *avoidable* unclarity is to ask him to specify the possible situations that would make his statement true. For instance, if a witness to a car accident says in court 'I was driving faster than usual' it would be reasonable to ask him whether, say, 60 mph counts for him as 'faster than usual', and if not whether 70 mph so counts, and so on. This is in effect a way of getting him to say more precisely than he initially did what he meant all along, by specifying of certain possible situations – for example, one in which he was driving at 60 mph, or one in which he was driving at 70 mph – whether or not each of them makes his sentence true. If his responses to enough such questions are consistent then we shall find it natural to call them clarifications of what he had meant all along by 'faster than usual'.

But if *that* is how we ascertain what someone really means, then it is also natural to think that somebody who *can't* answer such clarifying questions *doesn't* know what he means. Certainly this response would be reasonable in some cases. Suppose I say 'The ground was quite covered with plants.' Then you ask me 'Do spider plants count as "plants"?', 'Do geraniums count as "plants"?', and so on. But to each question I don't answer yes or no; I just say 'I don't know whether *they* are plants, I just mean that it was quite covered *with plants*.' If for enough species of plants (or other living things) I cannot say whether or not it counts as a 'plant' as I initially meant that word, it will be safe to conclude that I didn't know *what* I meant when I said that the ground was quite covered with 'plants'.

But while it is true that a *sufficiently* porous concept, as we might call it, is not really a concept at all, it doesn't follow that in order to mean anything at all I must be able to stop *all* such gaps (cf. PI 99). Consider again the example of the witness to the car accident. The barrister asks him 'What exactly counts for you as "faster than usual"? Does 60 mph count?' – Yes. 'Does 50 mph count?' – No. 'Does 55 mph count?' – Yes. 'Well then, does 52.5 mph count for you as "faster than usual"?' Here we can imagine the witness saying that he doesn't know. But this is not because he didn't know *what he meant all along*, but because he didn't mean anything *more precise* than what he had already said. To think the former would be to apply an everyday criterion for 'not knowing what one meant' with a nicety that is quite inappropriate. The temptation to do so is what lies behind the interlocutor's objection at PI 70.

(ii) Wittgenstein's discussion of the second objection is equally brief and rhetorical; but again there is a good deal more to be said.

> Frege compares a concept to an area and says that an area with vague boundaries cannot be called an area at all. This presumably means that we cannot do anything with it. – But is it senseless to say: "Stand roughly there"? (PI 71)

Of course it is *not* senseless; of course we *can* do something with it. But this does not really deal with the best reason for thinking that vague concepts are unusable, which is as follows.

It is of the essence of many vague concepts – because it is essential for our use of them – that their application is in optimal circumstances assessable solely on an observational basis. To put it more plainly: in optimal circumstances (good light, good eyesight, etc.) I can tell that something is red *just by looking*; I can tell whether you are standing roughly over there just by looking; I can tell whether a siren is loud just by listening; I can tell whether a rose is fragrant just by smelling, and so on. And if I *cannot* tell by such means, then nothing *else* is going to settle it. If a book has a cover that I hesitate to class as either 'red' or 'not red' then neither looking at any other thing nor any other sort of inquiry is going to settle it for me.

Now vague concepts that have this feature will also have another one: that one cannot consistently apply the concept to just one of two objects that are observationally indistinguishable, at least along the dimension that determines its application. For instance, one could not say in optimal circumstances of two visible but chromatically indistinguishable balls that one was red without agreeing that the other one was too. Doing so would be inconsistent with the condition that you can tell whether a ball is red just by looking. Since looking tells us the same whichever ball we look at, if it tells us that one ball is red then it tells us that the other ball is red too. Notice that I am not just saying that one cannot affirm that one ball is red while *denying* that the other one is. I am saying something stronger than that: one cannot even affirm that one ball is red while *withholding judgement* on the other. Even *that* would be inconsistent with the condition that you can tell whether a ball is red just by looking.

Now among the concepts that have this feature there are some that have this further one: that there is a finite sequence of objects, of which the first definitely is and the last definitely is not an instance of the concept, but such that no object in the sequence is observationally distinguishable from its successor along the dimension that determines the application of the concept (except obviously the last one, which *has* no successor). For instance, we might imagine a sequence of coloured balls of which the first is clearly red and the last is clearly green. The balls are so arranged that the reflectance properties of the surface of each ball are very slightly different from those of its predecessor – too slightly to register as a visible difference in colour. So balls that are adjacent in this sequence are chromatically indistinguishable. Let us call such a sequence a *Sorites sequence*.

We are finally in a position to see why vague concepts that satisfy these conditions, and many propositions that involve them, might after all be unusable. The difficulty is that given a Sorites sequence we can easily get a competent user of the corresponding vague concept to contradict himself. For instance, somebody who accepts that the first member of the sequence of balls is red will have to say the same of the second one. But if he says it of the second one then he will have to say it of the third one . . . until in the end he finds himself saying of a visibly *green* ball that *it* is red!

Or consider Wittgenstein's own example. If your standing on – that is, your centre of gravity's being directly above – a point on the surface of the Earth counts as obedience to what I meant when I said 'Stand roughly there', then so does your standing on a point that is 1 nm (1×10^{-9}m) to the north of it. But then a lengthy argument shows that if I say 'Stand roughly there', pointing at the region around the base of Nelson's Column in London, you could comply with my order by standing at the North Pole. The same point applies to ethical concepts, at least if they too admit of a continuum of intermediate cases (as Wittgenstein seems to think: PI 77a): if it is all right to touch somebody's elbow with your little finger then it is all right to sleep with her. And so on.

Here we come close to the idea which Frege had, and which one can find so hard to grasp, that the use of vague expressions is fundamentally incoherent. One may be inclined to dismiss Frege's idea as a mere prejudice if one does not reflect on examples such as these. (Dummett 1975b: 262)

In short it is their liability to generate contradictions that makes vague concepts unusable. Nothing in the *Philosophical Investigations* discussion of vagueness directly addresses this point.

However it is evident from certain of his other writings what Wittgenstein *would* have said to anyone who pressed it against him. He would have said that the *possibility* of deriving a contradiction from certain rules does *not* make those rules unusable if we do not *in fact* derive the contradiction.

[S]uppose that there is a contradiction in the statutes of a particular country. There might be a statute that on feast days the vice-president had to sit next to the president, and another statute that he had to sit between two ladies. This contradiction may remain unnoticed for some time, if he is constantly ill on feast-days. But one day a feast comes and he is not ill. Then what do we do? I may say, "We must get rid of this contradiction." All right, but does that vitiate what we did before? Not at all. (LFM 210)

In real life nobody ever *does* come across Sorites sequences; or if anyone does he does not base any practical conclusions upon the application of vague concepts to them. So in real life vague concepts *are* perfectly usable, even though a blindly mechanical application of them to such sequences *would* be of no use to us.

It is worth making two brief points about that. First, Wittgenstein's analogy of statutes can be somewhat misleading, for it gives the impression that *any* inconsistent set of rules and axioms is not thereby unusable so long as we do not derive the contradiction itself (cf. the exchange with Turing at LFM 220). But that is just not true: if a set of sentences is inconsistent then you can successively derive both a statement and its negation from it without ever proceeding via an explicit contradiction. But this point is immaterial to the case at hand: so long as either vague concepts are not in fact applied to Sorites sequences, or the results of doing so are disregarded, nothing stands in the way of saying that such concepts are usable. After all, they are *used*.

Second, beneath the somewhat bland pragmatism that I am here attributing to Wittgenstein there may be a deeper reason for rejecting the inference from inconsistency to unusability. For as we shall see, he can seem to be saying that a blind mechanical application of whatever rules govern the employment of my concepts is not a way of revealing something that was hidden all along within them. So in particular the deriving of a contradiction from them does not show that something was wrong with my rules *all along*. 'For I want to say "and it stops being a game" – not: "and now we see that it wasn't a game"' (RFM III-77). I shall return to the matter at 3.4.2.

(iii) It is easy to think of the grasping of a concept in terms of a visual metaphor. This manifests itself in everyday turns of phrase: when you grasp, for example, the colour concept 'yellow ochre' you may be said to *see what is common* to all of its instances. It is only slightly harder to take such turns of phrase literally and to think that when one grasps a word one becomes acquainted with an object of introspection. This inner object then gets *compared* with outer ones in order to settle the application of a word: in the case (e.g.) of 'yellow ochre' it applies to whatever outer object chromatically matches one's 'inner sample'. But if that is what happens when one grasps colour terms, how *can* they be vague? After all, it is not a vague matter whether or not this colour that I see here is or is not a match for the inner object that I associate with the term 'yellow ochre'.

Wittgenstein is later going to attack the very idea of an 'inner object' of introspection, cognizance of which constitutes your grasp of, say, a colour term (see, for example, PI 293, discussed at 4.1.3). But at this point he answers in another way. He says: suppose that there was such an inner object and consider how it would work for colours that admitted of *many shades* (say, blue or green). In that case there is typically no question of a chromatic *match* between the inner sample and the outer object: for green to admit of different shades *is* for a range of chromatically *distinguishable* items to fall under it. So the mere *having* of an inner sample of green is not going to be of any use to me. *It* does not settle precisely what does, and what does not, fall under the term 'green' as I understand it. To do that I need in addition to have some policy of how to use it; in particular some policy of saying that 'green' applies to something if and only if the latter lies within such-and-such a chromatic *range* of my sample.

Which shade is the 'sample in my mind' of the colour green – the sample of what is common to all shades of green?
"But might there not be such 'general' samples? Say a . . . sample of *pure* green?" – Certainly there might. But . . . for a slip of pure green to be understood as a sample of all that is greenish and not as a sample of pure green – this in turn resides in the way the samples are used. (PI 73)

Far from eliminating the vagueness of 'green' this analysis of my grasp of that term merely relocates it: for if I *do* use the sample as a sample of 'all that is greenish' then my judgements of whether something resembles that sample enough to be called 'green' itself will inevitably admit of borderline cases.

The argument so far has been that the mere presence in my mind – or for that matter on a piece of paper – of a sample associated with 'green' is not going to tell me how to apply it. But while this may seem to be true of that kind of sample there may also seem to be other sorts of sample that *do* intimate their application to an observer. The cases that I have in mind are those in which you see something *as* something: what Wittgenstein elsewhere calls cases of aspect-perception (PI pp. 165–6/193–4). A good example is the drawing on PI p. 166/194 of a 'duck-rabbit': an object that can appear either as a duck *or* as a rabbit; and here it looks as though I am describing a difference in the sorts of visual experience that it can produce. Or again one can see a squiggly line *as* a handwritten word; and on the one hand this appears to be a sort of experience (see examples (c) and (d) at PI p. 169/198); but on the other hand someone who sees it *as* such will regard a certain range of other patterns as resembling it; whereas someone who just sees the squiggly line will see no resemblance between tokens of (e.g.) the word 'pleasure' that are written in two very different hands. Now couldn't it happen in a similar way that one sees a sample of green *as* a sample of 'all that is greenish' rather than *as* a sample of pure green – one only attends, so to speak, to the greenish aspect of it? On the one hand this would seem to be a sort of experience. And on the other hand it would seem to be one that directs your policy.

Wittgenstein admits that such a thing might happen:

> Of course, there is such a thing as seeing in *this* way or *that*;
> and there are also cases where whoever sees a sample like *this*
> will in general use it in *this* way, and whoever sees it otherwise
> in another way. (PI 74)

But he insists that this 'seeing' of the sample in a certain way is
only *contingently* related to the use to which you then put it. He
does so in connection with a different example: the idea that one
might use an 'inner sample' of a leaf as a sample of *leaf-shapes
in general* because of the way in which one sees it:

> [T]he idea that if you see this leaf as a sample of 'leaf shape
> in general' you *see* it differently from someone who regards it
> as, say, a sample of this particular shape. Now this may well
> be so – though it is not so – for it would only be to say that, as
> a matter of experience, if you *see* the leaf in a particular way,
> you use it in such-and-such a way or according to such-and-
> such rules. (PI 74)

Here Wittgenstein's point appears to be that seeing a leaf, say, as
a sample of leaf-shapes in general is not yet to know how to
apply it: *it* is just an experience, and how one goes on to use it is
still up to you. On this point he appears to agree with his earlier
self (TLP 5.5423) but not with some of the things that he says in
the subtler exploration of these phenomena at *Philosophical
Investigations* II, xi. Consider this passage:

> If I saw the duck-rabbit as a rabbit, then I saw: these shapes
> and colours (I give them in detail) – and I saw besides some-
> thing like this: and here I point to a number of different
> pictures of rabbits. – This shews the difference between the
> concepts.
>   'Seeing as . . .' is not part of perception. And for that
> reason it is like seeing and again not like. (PI p. 168/196–7)

Here it looks as though seeing something *as* something is less a
matter of *what* one sees and more a matter of how one treats it
(e.g. what one points to in order to describe what one saw).

In that case, the connection between (a) seeing a sample as such-and-such and (b) using it to classify other objects as relevantly like or unlike it, is not adventitious but conceptual: to see an inner sample as (e.g.) a sample of a cube, of a leaf-shape in general or of all that is greenish, *is* in part to classify these things and not those as relevantly like it: as cubes, leaf-shaped objects or green things.

It may therefore be that the remarks on aspect-perception in the later part of the book can after all be developed into a partial defence of the tendency, noted at the beginning of this section, to assimilate understanding to seeing. Instead of doing so I merely note here that success in that project would do nothing to save Wittgenstein's main target in the material around PI 74. That was the idea that no 'inner' (or 'outer') sample can eliminate vagueness in the application of a concept. For even if seeing the shape of a leaf *as* a sample of leaf-shape in general is somehow an experience that simultaneously guides my policy of classification, there is still no reason to expect that it will recommend a definite verdict in every case. On the contrary, although I will be certainly inclined to consider the 'general leaf-shape' to be relevantly like some things and not relevantly like others, borderline cases will remain too.

(b) Wittgenstein also attempts to deal with the idea that whether or not we do in fact use vague expression, we *should* not do so. He makes two important points in this connection.

The first is that greater precision of expression can often be pointless. It all depends on what you want to *do* with the proposition or concept that you are making more precise.

> If I tell someone "Stand roughly here" – may not this explanation work perfectly? And may not [any] other one fail too?
>
> But isn't it an inexact explanation? – Yes; why shouldn't we call it "inexact"? Only let us understand what "inexact" means. For it does not mean "unusable". And let us consider what we call an "exact" explanation in contrast with this one. Perhaps something like drawing a chalk line round an area? Here it strikes us at once that the line has breadth. So a colour-edge would be more exact. But has this exactness still got a function here: isn't the engine idling? (PI 88a–b)

It is very easy to imagine situations in which the *point* of saying 'Stand roughly here' would not be served any better by a specification of the desired region that used colour-edges than by one that used a chalk line (this would be the case, for instance, if the person saying it was a bowler in a cricket team instructing one of his fielders).

That is obviously right and calls for little comment; but the second point is rather less plausible.

> "Inexact" is really a reproach, and "exact" is praise. And that is to say that what is inexact attains its goal less perfectly than what is more exact. Thus the point here is what we call "the goal". Am I inexact when I do not give our distance from the sun to the nearest foot, or tell a joiner the width of a table to the nearest thousandth of an inch?
>
> No *single* ideal of exactness has been laid down; we do not know what we are supposed to imagine under this head – unless you yourself lay down what is to be so called. But you will find it difficult to hit upon such a convention; at least any that satisfies you. (PI 88d–e)

The argument seems to be that (a) one cannot reproach, for example, a measurement for being inexact unless one has a concept of the *ideal* of exactness. But (b) we *have* no such concept – that is, we do not know what would count as an unimprovable degree of precision.

But there are two obvious responses to this. The first is that even if both points were true of the case of measurement, it is not clear that point (b) is true of the case that more immediately concerns us, that is, propositions. We might say that a proposition is inexact if one cannot draw a definite boundary around its truth-conditions, that is, if there is no one set of possible worlds consisting of *all and only* those situations in which it is *true*, the others comprising all and only the possible situations in which it is *false*. And so a proposition may be regarded as perfectly exact if it conforms to the ideal of the *Tractatus*: every possible situation is either one that makes it true or one that makes it false: there are no borderline cases. It may be true that in fact our thoughts do not conform to this ideal; but the ideal is still there.

And the second response is to question (a). It may seem an odd state to be in, but there seems to be no *incoherence* in always preferring more exact to less exact methods of measurement even if you have no conception of what unimprovable precision would be like (compare: always preferring the bigger of two numbers). Of course one would need to grasp the relation that holds between two methods of measurement when one is *more* precise than the other; but Wittgenstein is not expressing any doubts about *that*.

The importance of the general preference for precision perhaps lies not so much in Wittgenstein's treatment of it at PI 88 as in his regarding it as symptomatic of a certain conception – or rather, as he now thinks, misconception – of the nature and task of philosophy itself. We turn now to his treatment of that subject.

2.3. The nature of philosophy

Of all the subjects of which *Philosophical Investigations* treats, this is probably the one on which its views have the most in common with those of the *Tractatus*. However there are also points of disagreement, as is evident from the preceding discussion of PI 88. Here I discuss both continuities and differences in connection with the idea that philosophy is a body of activity and not a doctrine, aimed at revealing the nonsensicality of what philosophers had traditionally taken their subject to be.

In the *Tractatus* Wittgenstein had maintained that philosophy was not a body of empirical or *a priori* doctrine but a form of activity (TLP 4.111–4.112). Its task was not to help us to answer questions with which science can also help us; its task was rather to set limits to what science can say, or – what he then thought amounted to the same thing – to what can be *thought* (TLP 4.113–4.114).

In fact the claim that philosophy must at least *include* activities as well as doctrine follows from this conception of its task on the *Tractatus*'s own theory of meaning. Philosophy can only *state* the limits of thought and language by means of propositions that generalize over *all* propositions, including themselves. But

> No proposition can make a statement about itself, because a propositional sign cannot be contained in itself (that is the whole of the 'theory of types'). (TLP 3.332)

For instance, suppose that some proposition asserted *that all propositions are pictures* (TLP 4.021). If that proposition is to have the generality that is necessary for setting a limit to what can be thought, it must apply to itself. So it must be saying among other things that the proposition *that all propositions are pictures* is itself a picture. Now consider the two occurrences of the functional sign *x is a picture* in the proposition *that the proposition that all propositions are pictures is itself a picture*. Any sign, Wittgenstein says, contains a syntactic specification of all the meaningful substitutions for *x*, that is, a specification of what signs can be substituted for *x* (compare the sign *n + 2 = m*, where the use of the expressions *n* and *m* might conventionally be taken to indicate that only Arabic numerals can be substituted for them). But this means that the sign cannot *itself* be among those substitutions:

> In logical syntax the meaning of a sign should never play a role. It must be possible to establish logical syntax without mentioning the *meaning* of a sign: only the description of expressions may be presupposed. (TLP 3.33)

> The reason why a function cannot be its own argument is that the sign for a function already contains the prototype of its argument, and it cannot contain itself. (TLP 3.333)

And it follows that if the proposition *that the proposition that all propositions are pictures is itself a picture* says anything at all, the two occurrences in it of *x is a picture* must be occurrences of *different* signs, since the first sign cannot contain itself, whereas the second sign clearly *can* – because in this propositional sign it *does* – contain the first sign. Since therefore they admit of different substitution instances they must be *different* signs. (This is the linguistic counterpart of TLP 2.0213.) But then our proposition is *not* making a suitably general claim: it does not say of itself what it tries to say of everything else, any more than ' "The only thing that deters hardened criminals is a long sentence" is a long sentence' says of 'The only thing that deters hardened criminals' what the latter says of the only thing that determines hardened criminals. So our proposition has misfired: if it made a claim at all it was not the one that was intended.

Thus in order to achieve the aim of philosophy we must resort not to *stating* the limit of thought but to *showing* others that their assertions have crossed that limit.

The correct method in philosophy would really be the following: to say nothing except what can be said, i.e. propositions of natural science – i.e. something that has nothing to do with philosophy – and then, whenever someone else wanted to say something metaphysical, to demonstrate to him that he had failed to give a meaning to certain signs in his propositions. (TLP 6.53)

This activity of demonstrating 'that he had failed to give a meaning' to certain signs is what philosophers who have read the *Tractatus* ought to be doing to anyone who tries to 'say something metaphysical'.

Now in *Philosophical Investigations* he rejects that earlier reason for thinking that these truths cannot be stated. For he no longer thinks that the meaning of a sign must be laid down once and for all. He now thinks on the contrary that there may be continuities between different patterns of use, so that by *extending* the use of a sign to cover new cases one might still be keeping faith with its old meaning. This might happen, for example, when people who initially applied the word 'pain' only to living things then began applying it to dolls (cf. PI 282); or when people who initially thought that only visible operations on paper counted as 'calculations' then began to recognize an activity of 'calculating in the head' (cf. PI 364, 385–6). Equally then, somebody who had used the word 'proposition' to apply only to a limited range of sentences might with similar fidelity to what he already meant begin to apply it to a wider range of sentences. (I discuss the application of this point to sensation ascriptions at 4.2.6.)

But although he no longer has this reason for doing so, he continues to accept that philosophy is the activity of showing people who scratch their heads over metaphysical doctrines that they really are nonsensical:

The results of philosophy are the uncovering of one or another piece of plain nonsense and bumps that the understanding has got by running its head up against the limits of language. (PI 119)

If one tried to advance *theses* in philosophy, it would never be possible to debate them, because everyone would agree to them. (PI 128)

The reason for recommending this activity is that the philosophical talk it is directed against is itself an activity in which language really has no function – what appears to be meaningful (because grammatically well-formed) sentences are truly meaningless because they have no use at all:

> When philosophers use a word – "knowledge", "being", "object", "I", "proposition", "name" – and try to grasp the *essence* of the thing, one must always ask oneself: is the word ever actually used in this way in the language which is its original home? –
>
> What *we* do is to bring words back from their metaphysical to their everyday use. (PI 116)

So what the philosopher ought to do is this: faced with someone who wonders whether, for example, all words are names, or whether space is necessarily three-dimensional, one does not endorse or oppose that thesis, one *reminds* him of our *ordinary* use of the expressions 'word', 'name', 'space', and so on and then he sees that his sentence is really meaningless. 'The work of the philosopher consists in assembling reminders for a particular purpose' (PI 127).

What are we to make of this? It can certainly *appear* that philosophical claims of any great generality are just meaningless. Continuing with the example 'All words are names': if somebody said that in a philosophical context it would not be clear at once just what he meant by it. And Wittgenstein is surely correct that this is because he is using the word 'names' in a way that is very distant from its non-philosophical uses. So somebody who had only learnt to use the word 'name' in non-philosophical contexts ('What are the names of these children?'; 'Everybody whose name begins with "S" step forward') might well find himself at a loss in face of the general Augustinian thesis.

But why should the correct response to this be to *give up* on the philosophical claim? Why couldn't one admit that without further explanation one only has a hazy idea of what it means, but then instead of giving up try to *give* it a meaning whose truth one could then test?

Obviously one couldn't give it any meaning one liked, or at least not if one wished to maintain that one was expressing a philosophical thesis. If I announce that by 'All words are names' I am going to mean what everyone else means by 'Pigs fly', and then conclude that 'All words are names' is false, nobody is going to think that I have said anything of relevance to philosophy. But in contrast with this case there *are* ways of making a word precise that can be said to keep faith with our possibly hazy everyday understanding.

Thus scientific enquiry frequently gives words some precise meaning that emphasizes just *one* of the many criteria that unsystematically settle everyday usage depending on the purpose at hand. For instance, somebody who wishes to measure changes in 'the income of a nation' cannot be content with the ordinary word 'income' because of its vagueness; he has to replace it with some such specific notion as GDP, that is, some measurable variable that captures at least some of the things about income that made the initial question worth caring about. Of course that variable may not encompass *everything* that concerned him about income in the first place, and it may encompass other things too; but then he is free to devise other variables that will improve his coverage, for example, GNP. One could not object that by so defining 'income' our economist has departed from ordinary usage to such an extent as to make his enquiry point-less (which is what happened in the case of 'Pigs fly'). On the contrary what he has done is to *isolate* the point (or better: one of the points) of asking after changes in income.

Now why can we not do the same in philosophy? Return to the thesis that all words are names. Thus baldly stated it means nothing: but why can't we simply *specify* the things that we might mean by 'names' in this context and then go on to test the result-ing theory? In fact that was just what I tried very perfunctorily to do: in chapter 1 I suggested three relatively precise meanings for or consequences of that thesis – 'all words have the same function', 'all words are learnt by ostension', 'all words mean just what they denote' – and tried to learn in light of Wittgenstein's own remarks which were true and which were false. Why doesn't that count as a way of *advancing* philosophical theses and also as a way of *settling* them?

One objection to this idea of philosophy is that it would give many philosophical theses an empirical interpretation. For instance, the sentence 'all words are names' might get interpreted as the empirical thesis that we learn all words by ostensive definition. Or the thesis that space is necessarily three-dimensional might get interpreted as a question that only an empirically supported physical theory can answer. But (the objector will continue) philosophical theses are *not* empirical (and therefore typically contingent) theses but rather *a priori* truths (if they are truths at all) discoverable from the armchair (cf. PI 109).

But why think that? Only on a very narrow conception of philosophy could one say that it made no empirical claims. To take four examples that are very distant from one another in time as well as doctrine: Aristotle (in *De Anima*), Berkeley (in the *New Theory of Vision*), Marx (in *Capital*) and Russell (in *The Analysis of Mind*) were all engaged in philosophical enquiries that resulted in empirical (and simultaneously philosophical) claims. Who is Wittgenstein to tell them that they are not doing philosophy? Or again, why should we *not* say that fundamental metaphysical questions concerning space and time are in fact the province of physics as well as philosophy? Who is Wittgenstein to tell us that Newton's theory, or Einstein's, were not advances that did more for our *philosophical* understanding of space, time and matter than centuries of purely *a priori* theorizing?

In connection with time Wittgenstein remarks:

Augustine says in the *Confessions* ["What, then, is time? If nobody asks me, I know well enough what it is; but if I am asked what it is and try to explain, I am baffled."] – This could not be said about a question of natural science ("What is the specific gravity of hydrogen?" for instance). Something that we know when no one asks us, but no longer know when we are supposed to give an account of it, is something that we need to *remind* ourselves of. (PI 89)

We feel as if we had to *penetrate* phenomena: our investigation, however, is directed not towards phenomena, but, as one might say, towards the '*possibilities*' of phenomena. We remind our-selves, that is to say, of the *kind of statement* that we make about phenomena. Thus Augustine recalls to mind the differ-ent statements that are made about the duration, past, present or future, of events. (PI 90)

I confess to finding this attitude incomprehensible. I myself don't know what time is *whether or not* you ask me; but if I knew its role in an empirically justified physical theory I *should* know well enough what it was. And the same goes for space, and colour, and the mind, and language.

It seems to me that the distance between Wittgenstein's conception of philosophy and this rival conception of it is so great that perhaps they ought not to be reckoned rivals at all. The truth is that here we have two completely different activities: trying to answer very general questions about man and the universe while frankly admitting that empirical findings will often be relevant to this; and reminding ourselves *a priori* of the ordinary uses of words to stop ourselves from getting enmeshed in confusions. Both activities are legitimate; and in the end it doesn't much matter which one gets to be called 'philosophy'. He himself once said:

If, e.g., we call our investigations "philosophy", this title, on the one hand, seems appropriate, on the other hand it has certainly misled people. (One might say that the subject we are dealing with is one of the heirs of the subject which used to be called "philosophy".) (BB 28)

But the subject that tries to find answers to specific philosophical questions – or at least to artificial formulations of them – is another heir, and it is the one that most philosophers in the Western tradition pursue today. What justifies the continued study of Wittgenstein for *them* is that – intentionally or not – much of what he had to say sheds light upon their problems too.

2.4. PI 134–7: The 'general form of the proposition'

The picture of language that had held captive the author of the *Tractatus* appeared at 4.5 of that book: 'The general form of a proposition is: This is how things stand.' Now this expression

'This is how things stand' is something that he had got 'from everyday language and nowhere else' (PI 134); and Wittgenstein now applies the method of PI 116 by asking: what is its use in everyday language?

Well, it is true that 'This is how things stand' has a kind of generality that enables it to stand in for any proposition: we can always say, 'He said p; that is, he said that that is how things stand'; and what follows the semicolon here just repeats what preceded it, whatever p is (PI 134b). But the fact that this sort of generality attaches to 'This is how things stand' does *not* mean that its use at *Tractatus* 4.5 *tells* us anything about what a proposition is. That is: if an alien who visited Earth and asked to be shown which bits of language expressed propositions, it would not do tell him – They are the ones of the form 'This is how things stand.'

The reason it wouldn't do is that you need *already* to know which bits of language express propositions – or better, which ones you are prepared to call 'propositions' – *before* you can say which ones are of the form 'This is how things stand.' It is as if somebody were to explain what an Arabic numeral is by saying that any Arabic numeral can be meaningfully substituted for the '2' in '121'. It is true, but it doesn't specify any means of telling *whether* anything is an Arabic numeral: rather all it says is that given the Arabic numerals – of which '2' is one – the 'game' that we play with them licenses this substitution.

The same point applies to a related idea: that the essence of a proposition – its making a claim on reality – is captured by saying that it is the sort of thing that can be *true or false* – as opposed, say, to an exclamation, a sneeze or a hat. Again Wittgenstein argues that this only seems to tell us anything. For truth is not a special relation that propositions have to reality; it is rather that 'p is true' is just a way of saying whatever 'p' does; and 'p is false' is just a way of saying what '~p' says (PI 136). But we cannot decide what belongs to that class by first assembling a collection of words and then asking whether truth and falsity somehow 'fit' that assembly, as one jigsaw piece might fit another; it is rather that 'we only predicate "true" and "false" of what we call a proposition' (ibid.).

So while both 'being true or false' and 'being of the form: This is how things stand' do indeed specify necessary and sufficient conditions on propositionhood, they do not specify any feature common to all propositions in virtue of which we call them propositions; nor do they specify any feature that we could identify prior to having identified the propositions themselves.

Two things follow from this: first, that 'proposition' may well express a family resemblance concept. At any rate the existence of *these* necessary and sufficient conditions on propositionhood does nothing to show otherwise. That is why Wittgenstein says:

> But haven't we got a concept of what a proposition is, of what we take "proposition" to mean? – Yes, just as we also have a concept of what we mean by "game". (PI 135)

The second thing that follows is that the supposed insight behind the *Tractatus* was not really that but merely a move within our grammar. It had seemed both profound and mysterious that there are such things as propositions, that is, items that are somehow able to do so much as *lay a claim* upon reality, to reach right up to it and say '*this – is – so*' (PI 95). But saying that that is what they do is just offering a paraphrase, not describing a deep connection in reality. It is not that somehow we have invested certain spoken or written items with a magical power that nobody quite understands. Instead, it is just of the things that we *call* 'propositions' that we feel able to *say* that they 'make a claim on reality', 'reach up to it', and the rest. Wittgenstein's later accusation of the solipsist can with greater justice be directed at *Tractatus* 4.5: 'You interpret a grammatical movement made by yourself as a quasi-physical phenomenon which you are observing' (PI 401).

SECTION 3. MEANING AND UNDERSTANDING

Wittgenstein pivots upon the notion of fitting discussed at PI 136–7 to begin an extended discussion of understanding and meaning that constitutes the heart of *Philosophical Investigations*. Somebody might say that the use of a word 'fits' its meaning; and you *would* say this if you thought that the meaning of a word is *not* the use itself (as proposed at PI 43) but rather something that *guides* the use. And that is surely a very natural thought if you reflect upon what happens when you *suddenly* understand something. For you seem to grasp it in a flash, 'and what we grasp in this way is surely something different from the 'use' which is extended in time' (PI 138). It is this idea of grasping something in a flash that will preoccupy Wittgenstein in the next 50-odd sections.

3.1. The cube

But what *does* occur to you when you grasp something in a flash? Wittgenstein first considers the suggestion that it is a mental picture (PI 139c). Before discussing what he says about this it is worth noting one distinctive and interesting feature of many of his discussions of 'mental pictures' or 'inner images': whenever he considers their function he thinks that it makes no difference whether he considers inner or outer pictures.

> We could perfectly well, for our purposes, replace every process of imagining by a process of looking at an object or by painting, drawing or modeling and every process of speaking to oneself by speaking aloud or writing. (BB 4; cf. PI 141b)

Thus what he says, for example, about the inner image of a cube at PI 139 applies at least as well to a drawing of a cube on a piece of paper. The strategy is really just a way of taking seriously the picture of 'inner' images or activities. For such inner objects, states, events and processes are modelled upon their outer counterparts; both the point and the ultimate downfall of these models is that we are 'transposing an essentially third-person situation into some kind of mental interior' (Moran 2003: 2).

3.1.1. The picture and its projection

Wittgenstein's actual discussion of the 'mental image' proposal centres upon the example of the word 'cube'. Could it be that when I suddenly come to understand the word 'cube', what occurs to me is an inner picture of a cube? At PI 139 he does not deny that one could call this picture the meaning of the word 'cube', so that the meaning *has* come before my mind when I understood 'cube' for the first time. What he denies is that just one pattern of use *fits* the picture in the way that just one jigsaw piece fits another.

Why not? Because if one use of the word 'cube' can be said to fit the picture that then came before my mind, so too could another.

> Perhaps you say: "It's quite simple; – if that picture occurs to me and I point to a triangular prism for instance, and say it is a cube, then this use of the word doesn't fit the picture." – But doesn't it fit? I have purposely so chosen the example that it is quite easy to imagine a *method of projection* according to which the picture does fit after all. (PI 139)

By 'a method of projection' here Wittgenstein means something like this: suppose that one had some method of drawing imaginary 'projection lines' connecting certain points on the surface of the pictured cube to points on the surface of a physical object. (Here one really has to think of a picture on paper, or even a three-dimensional model.) If by some application of that method the points of the pictured cube can be matched one-to-one with points on the physical object, we shall apply the word 'cube' to the latter. And now his point is that nothing in the picture itself 'fits' any particular *way* of drawing such lines. For instance, if I always drew lines from the vertices of the pictured cube to the vertices of the physical object, then obviously I'd only apply the word 'cube' to objects which themselves had eight vertices, so I'd apply the word to cubes[11] but not to triangular prisms. But what if I practiced instead a method of drawing lines from each *face* of the pictured cube to the *vertices* of the physical object? In that case a triangular prism *would* 'fit' the picture that I had associated with 'cube', for it has six vertices and a cube has six faces.

There is an obvious way to modify the idea that might seem to get around this objection. This is to suppose that the inner picture associated with 'cube' depicts not only the cube itself but also an appropriate method of projection. Thus imagine that the inner picture associated with 'cube' consisted of two pictured cubes, together with 'lines of projection' passing from the vertices of the one to the vertices of the other. Wouldn't this rule out my applying 'cube' to triangular prisms?

'But does this really get me any further? Can't I now imagine different applications of this schema too?' The answer is that you can: nothing in this more complicated picture tells you how to project *it* onto one or another application of the word 'cube' (PI 141). For instance, what is there in the picture that settles how I am to compare the pictured lines of projection with the imaginary ones that connect one of the pictured cubes to a physical object? If each imaginary projection line is meant to have the *same* origin as a pictured projection line (i.e. a vertex of one of the cubes) then of course I will have a method of comparison that rules out my applying 'cube' to a triangular prism. But if each imaginary projection line is meant to have, say, an origin that is equidistant from four coplanar origins of pictured projection lines (i.e. a centre-point of one of the cube's faces), then my method of comparison will *not* rule out my so applying it. So this amendment does not get us anywhere: it looks as though my use of the word 'cube' cannot after all be said to fit or not to fit a picture that comes before my mind.

It is worth mentioning that this position resembles that in the *Tractatus*: or more precisely, what Wittgenstein says here about pictures is close to what he says in the *Tractatus* about *sentences* or *propositional signs*, which he thought *were* pictures. The mere presence before one's inner eye (or outer eye) of a propositional or pictorial sign cannot amount to an understanding of that picture because the picture cannot – for the reasons that we have just rehearsed – contain its own method of projection. But it is also the view of the *Tractatus* that to understand the picture in one way or another one must also perform a special kind of psychological activity: one must *think its sense*; doing this is what he calls 'projection' (TLP 3.11). To do so is to have a thought, that is, really to *mean* one thing rather than another by the picture. 'A propositional sign, applied and thought out, is a thought' (TLP 3.5).[12] One has then turned the propositional *sign* into a propositional *symbol*, that is, a sign together with its method of application (TLP 3.32).

We shall return to the *Tractatus* idea, that understanding a picture in some way is a psychological process that accompanies it, at 3.3; and at 4.2.3 we shall consider the further *Tractatus* idea that there must be a self or soul to carry out this process.

3.1.2. *'Extremely general facts of nature'*
People who have never been troubled by what is now troubling us have always found it quite natural to say that one can grasp

somebody's meaning in a flash, that the meaning of a word can come before one's mind, and all the rest. Does Wittgenstein want to prohibit these natural turns of phrase – or if not to prohibit them then at least to insist that they are no more *literally* true than 'The sun sets'? The answer to both questions is no. In response to the foregoing argument about projection he has the interlocutor say: 'Well yes, but then mayn't an *application come before my mind*? – It may [Wittgenstein replies]: only we need to get clearer about our application of *this* expression.' Later in the same section he continues:

> Can there be a collision between picture and application? There can, inasmuch as the picture makes us expect a different use, because people in general apply *this* picture like *this*. (PI 141)

But if there can be a collision then there can also be a fit; so contrary to the impression that PI 139 can give, Wittgenstein is *not* arguing that in no sense of 'fit' can one's use of the associated word be said to fit or fail to fit a picture in one's mind (or on paper). What he is arguing against is a certain misconception of what that fitting amounts to; the ordinary speaker is immune from this criticism in so far as he does not have that illegitimate sense in mind. Let us consider first what the illegitimate sense of fitting is, and then what the legitimate sense of fitting is.

The illegitimate idea is that the picture somehow *forces* an application upon us (PI 140), so that a use fits the picture not in virtue of its being a normal response to the picture (i.e. a typical way of using it) but *independently* of how we normally respond to it: so that, for example, if the same picture were to occur to a Martian in connection with the word 'cube', the same application of that word would thereby be laid down for him too (cf. PI p. 46 n. 2 (b)/54 n. (b)). It is against this conception of fitting that PI 139 was directed; and what it showed was that the application of the word 'cube' does not fit the associated picture in that rather demanding sense, because 'there are other processes, besides the one we originally thought of, which we should sometimes be prepared to call "applying the picture of a cube"' (PI 140).

But there is a second and less demanding sense in which a use may be said to fit a picture. He describes this at PI 141 in the words already quoted. The use that fits a picture is the use that we expect on the basis of people's actual application of the picture. They might have applied it in another way or in no coherent way at all. But as a matter of fact when you say to somebody 'Bring me something looking like this' while showing him a picture of a cube, he will bring you a *cube*. That is why we can say truly that somebody who diverges from this normal case – somebody who brings, for example, a triangular prism – is using the word 'cube' in a way that does *not* fit that picture.

Wittgenstein had already illustrated this sense in which one thing can 'fit' another:

> What about learning to determine the subject of a sentence by means of the question "Who or what . . .?" – Here, surely, there is such a thing as the subject's 'fitting' this question; for otherwise how should we find out what the subject was by means of the question? We find it out much as we find out which letter of the alphabet comes after 'K' by saying the alphabet up to 'K' to ourselves. Now in what sense does 'L' fit on to this series of letters? (PI 137)

'L' fits on to that series of letters in the sense that it comes *next in our alphabet*, that is, we customarily so arrange the letters of our alphabet that 'L' immediately succeeds 'K'. It is in the same sense that the use can be said to fit the meaning that 'comes before your mind' when you say 'cube' to yourself.

Let us now return to the issue that motivated this line of enquiry. It was an objection to the idea that meaning is use: no, it was said, meaning is not use but something *prior* to use that your use *fits*. And the reason for this was supposed to be that the *meaning* can come before your mind 'in a flash'; but how can the *use*, which is extended in time, come before your mind in such a flash?

Wittgenstein seems to me to have taught us two things about this. First, he is agreeing that the meaning *can* be a picture that comes before your mind, but that this will only happen when the *application* of the picture 'comes before your mind' too. And that is what will happen if you are prepared to use the picture as it is typically used. So the application, which is extended in time, *can* come before your mind after all. Understanding really *is* something that makes its appearance in a moment (PI 151). 'But how can the use, which is extended in time, appear to you all at once?' I shall return to that in a moment.

The second thing that he has taught us is this: the picture *is* something that the use can in a sense fit or fail to fit, but that is only *because* it has the use it does, that is, *because* people will (e.g.) fetch a cube when they are shown a picture of one and asked to fetch what is in the picture. So independently of the first point we can insist that use remains prior to meaning in the order of explanation. A use does not fit a picture because of the meaning that the picture already had; rather, a picture has the meaning that it does *because* of the use that we typically *give* it.

Let me conclude this section by briefly emphasizing two points that are important for an understanding of Wittgenstein's overall approach to problems of meaning and understanding. The first point is that his discussion at PI 139–41 illustrates the extent to which the existence of a concept relies upon contingent regularities. In particular the relation that 'fitting' expresses would not pick out anything at all if there happened not to *be* any typical reaction to a picture. If on one day I responded to the request to bring me something looking like this by bringing a triangular prism, and on another day I brought a cube; if on those occasions *you* responded in different ways too, and differently also from *me*; if no pattern emerged over a longer period of time or over a larger demographic cross-section: in that case we should attach no more sense to saying that a pattern of use 'fits' the picture than we do to saying that it 'fits' (e.g.) the weather.

As indicated by its exposition at PI 142 (see also p. 48/56n and p. 195/230), this is one instance of a very widespread, and for Wittgenstein very important, pattern of dependence of our concepts – that is, of our having words to express concepts – upon 'extremely general facts of nature' (p. 48/56n). Other examples in Wittgenstein's work are as follows: the distinction between certain and uncertain memories and its dependence upon the facts about their actual reliability (OC 632); the dependence of our arithmetical language upon general facts about the stability of physical objects (RFM I-37); and, as we shall see, the dependence of third-personal sensational ascriptions upon certain regularities in our means of *expressing* the latter (4.2.5).

75

And the second point is that if these very general facts do obtain, I don't think that Wittgenstein wants to stop anywhere short of saying that the occurrence of a mental image on an occasion can really *be* (on that occasion) the instantaneous onset of understanding. 'But how can the application, which is extended in time, occur to you all at once?' The answer is that for something to be 'the appearance before your mind of the application', for a mental event to *count* as that, is something that *depends* on very general facts that are spread out over time; but that event need not itself *be* spread out over time. Compare: a daub of paint on a canvas can *be* a painted smile; but its being one depends upon what is painted *elsewhere* on the canvas. (In another painting, that very daub would *not* have been a smile.) And yet it does not follow that the daub itself is spread all over the canvas.

3.2. Dispositions

Wittgenstein now turns to a new example. Suppose that we are trying to teach a pupil to use the system of Arabic numerals by showing him, and getting him to copy, initial segments of the number series in that notation: 0, 1, 2, 3, ... So we write down such sequences, and he writes them down after us, and when he gets it wrong we correct him. In all probability he will – if he is a normal human being – eventually master the system, that is, he will acquire our ability to write down *indefinitely* long segments of the number series.

How do we tell that he has mastered it? Well, by looking at what he does: if he continues the series correctly enough times without prompting, and if he can be made to see his errors for what they are and also to correct them – in that case we shall say with reasonable confidence that he has mastered the system.

But his mastery of the system cannot, it seems, *consist* in his having continued the series correctly up to, say, the hundredth place on some particular occasion. For his mastery of it extends *beyond* the hundredth place. Wittgenstein gives these two very clear expressions of that idea:

> Perhaps you will say here: to have got the system (or, again, to understand it) can't consist in continuing the series up to *this* or *that* number: *that* is only applying one's understanding.

The understanding itself is a state which is the *source* of the correct use. (PI 146)

Your idea, then, is that you know the application of the rule of the series quite apart from remembering actual applications to particular numbers. And you will perhaps say: "Of course! For the series is infinite and the bit of it that I can have developed finite." (PI 147)

Clearly the importance of this example is that it presents another temptation to distinguish how you *mean* something from how you *use* it, and more particularly: to distinguish one's understanding of a series from his actual development of it, because the former is infinite (or indefinite) and the latter is finite; so to *understand* the series must be a matter of being in a certain sort of mental state from which 'all our acts spring as from a reservoir' (BB 146).

Now a reservoir is there whether or not one is drawing water from it. And at PI 148 Wittgenstein asks whether our 'knowledge of the application of the rule' is present when it is not being exercised or even thought about. And an obvious reply would be that this knowledge or understanding is like one's knowledge of the ABC, or the multiplication tables: such a state *is* always present, because, it is thought, that state is a type of *disposition*.

3.2.1. *A-dispositions and B-dispositions*
In discussing Wittgenstein's treatment of this possibility at PI 149 we must distinguish two things that the word 'disposition' might mean. When one says that an object (say, a heated glass bowl) has a disposition to crack if placed in cold water, one might mean simply this: that if it *were* placed in cold water then it *would* crack. A heated glass bowl could have that disposition without *ever* being in cold water; but even if it *is* in cold water at some time it will have the property even at those other times when it is not. So for something to have a certain disposition in this sense is *just* for it to satisfy a certain condition about what would happen to it in certain hypothetical circumstances. Let us call this sort of feature an *A-disposition*.

Now for all that we have said about A-dispositions, two objects might differ only over *them*: there might, for example, be two glass bowls of exactly the same temperature and molecular structure, and in fact indiscernible in every respect *except* that if you were to put them both in cold water, one but not the other would crack. It would be very surprising if something like that did happen, because an object that has an A-disposition normally has it in virtue of some property that is *not* itself just a condition upon its behaviour in hypothetical circumstances, but an actual feature of the object. For instance, bits of salt have A-dispositions to dissolve (i.e. if you were to put this salt in water it would form a solution); but they do so in virtue of an underlying chemical structure that explains their dissolution. This actual feature of an object that underlies some one of its A-dispositions is often called the basis of that A-disposition: here I shall call it a *B-disposition*.

3.2.2. The first objection: PI 149

Let us now return to Wittgenstein's discussion of the idea that understanding the series, knowing one's multiplication table, and the like, are what he calls 'dispositions'. He writes:

> If one says that knowing the ABC is a state of the mind, one is thinking of a state of a mental apparatus (perhaps of the brain) by means of which we explain the *manifestations* of that knowledge. Such a state is called a disposition. (PI 149)

He is here using 'disposition' to denote the state that *explains* one's tendency to utter the ABC in response to the stimulus of a query; that is, he is using it to denote what I am calling a B-disposition. The postulated state corresponds to the molecular structure of the salt, not its hypothetical behaviour in water. And the proposal is that we identify the pupil's knowledge of the ABC (or understanding of the series) with the state of the mind or brain that explains its manifestations in his behaviour.
Wittgenstein criticizes the idea as follows:

> But there are objections to speaking of a state of the mind here, inasmuch as there ought to be two different criteria for such a state: a knowledge of the construction of the apparatus, quite apart from what it does. (PI 149)

What could this mean?

The difficulty seems to be that we cannot specify the state in question except as 'whatever it is that explains the pupil's reciting the ABC correctly' (or: 'whatever it is that explains his being able to continue the series on any occasion'). But why is *that* a difficulty with this realization of the 'reservoir' idea? Wittgenstein does not say: but here is a proposal.

Suppose that we made an exhaustive list of all the B-dispositions that could underlie an A-disposition towards the appropriate behaviour – in this case, the A-disposition that the pupil possesses if and only if he would, if asked, correctly recite the ABC. These would be properties of his brain or mind: records of how things *actually* are with him. The property of enjoying a red after-image might be one such item; the property of having neuron N firing at a rate R might be another. Then I am taking the proposal to be that if knowledge of the ABC is a state of the person then it is identical with some (possibly very complex) combination of properties on that list: whichever combination, that is, that best explains the A-disposition of interest.

Wittgenstein's objection is that knowledge of the ABC cannot be so identified because our *sole* criterion for settling whether someone possesses that knowledge is the *behavioural* manifestation and *not* the state that explains it in normal cases. Suppose that we found that among the human beings that we initially test, all and only those in brain-state N_1 were able to recite the ABC at will. Let us now see what happens if we identify the understanding with that brain-state (exactly the same points apply to any other B-dispositional 'state of the mind'). Suppose that we now find a group of people in whom brain-state N_1 does *not* underlie their A-disposition to recite the ABC if asked: people from this second group who are in N_1 frequently get it wrong. Rather, among people of this group it is possession of the brain-state N_2 that underlies it. I think we should all agree that among people from this second group it is those in brain-state N_2 and not those in brain-state N_1 who know their ABC. But the people in N_1 in the second group are in the same state as people from the first group who *do* know their ABC; knowledge of the ABC cannot therefore be a matter of one's being in any such B-dispositional state.

We may illustrate the point with a familiar contrast. We use the terms 'red' and 'blue' to denote surfaces that are A-disposed to produce impressions of red or blue upon normal observers in a range of normal conditions. If the surfaces that actually produce an impression of red (e.g. the surfaces of tomatoes) had instead produced an impression of blue, those very surfaces would have been *not* red, but *blue* (i.e. that is how actual people should describe this circumstance). By contrast we use the term 'water' to denote whatever chemical actually falls from the sky as rain, is clear and drinkable, and so on. That chemical is actually H_2O; but – and here is the contrast with 'red' and 'blue' – if that very stuff, that very H_2O had been opaque and poisonous, it would *still have been water*. So in the case of water, we have 'knowledge of the construction of the apparatus [from hydrogen and oxygen], quite apart from what it does [fall from the sky, fill lakes, etc.]'. So being composed of water is a state of something but being red is not; nor, for the same reason, is one's knowledge of the ABC, or one's understanding of a word, or one's being able to continue a numerical sequence.

Of course our use of 'understanding' 'knowing the ABC', and so on *might* have been different: those words might have resembled 'water' in just the respect that they actually resemble 'red'. In that case they would have been concepts that picked out states.

To see what sort of a difference that would involve, we need only compare the psychological concepts that we apply to human beings with the analogues that we apply to machines. A very revealing – because very straightforward – example is the concept of 'reading', by which Wittgenstein means not anything involving linguistic understanding but such processes as transcription and its converse of reading out loud; also sight-reading a musical score and turning a typescript into handwriting. (PI 156a). More generally we may call 'reading' any activity that involves deriving a reproduction in one format of an original that is in another (PI 162).

Let us consider the difference between (a) the grounds on which we say that a child who is learning some such activity has started to read and (b) the grounds on which we might say that a machine that is under construction – say, a pianola – has started to read. This example makes the difference very clear:

Human beings or creatures of some other kind are used by us as reading-machines. They are trained for this purpose.

The trainer says of some that they can already read, of others that they cannot yet do so. Take the case of a pupil who has so far not taken part in the training; if he is shewn a written word he will sometimes produce some sort of sound, and here and there it happens 'accidentally' to be roughly right. A third person hears this pupil on such an occasion and says "He is reading". But the teacher says: "No, he isn't reading; that was just an accident". – But let us suppose that this pupil continues to react correctly to further words that are put before him. After a while the teacher says: "Now he can read!" – But what of that first word? Is the teacher to say "I was wrong, and he *did* read it" – or: "He only began really to read later on"? – When did he begin to read? (PI 157)

It is the mark of the concept as applied *to human beings* that the question has no answer: the only facts that are relevant to settling it are facts about what the pupil did; and if *they* do not settle it then nothing remains *to* be settled. ('But surely it is a matter of *logic* that either he *was* reading or he *wasn't!*' I shall discuss this objection at 4.2.7.)

That is not how things stand with a *mechanical* reading device, for example, a pianola. This is a device that automatically plays music if you feed into it a metal plate on which the score is engraved. Suppose that while somebody is constructing it we keep feeding it with such plates. Now and again it emits a note that happens to be on the metal plate, but this is just an accident. A third person hearing this says 'Now it is reading music.' But we say 'No, it isn't reading; that was just an accident.' – But let us suppose that the machine continues to respond correctly to further scores that are fed into it. After a while we say: 'Now it can read!' – But what of that first note?

In this case, and in contrast to the case of the pupil, there *is* an answer to the question whether it was reading that note. For in the case of a pianola, it is not *only* what it does but *also* its internal construction by which we settle whether or not it is 'reading'. If the right wires were connected when we fed it that first note, it was reading even then; but if they were not, it was not reading.

When we speak of a *pianola*'s being able to read we are allowing for the identification of this state in some other way than the pianola's behaviour – 'a knowledge of the construction of the apparatus, quite apart from what it does'. But when we say it of a human being we do *not* allow for that possibility:

> But in the case of the living reading-machine "reading" meant reacting to written signs in such-and-such ways. This concept was therefore quite independent of that of a mental or other mechanism. (PI 157)

That is why being able to read is not really a type of mental *state* at all. And the concepts of 'knowing the ABC' and 'understanding the series' do not pick out states either. We cannot identify such knowledge or understanding with any B-disposition.

3.2.3. *The second objection: PI 158*
At PI 158 Wittgenstein appears to allude to another reason to be sceptical about identifying the ability to read with a B-disposition: what he says there is clearly just as applicable to the cases of understanding a series and knowing the ABC. He has just written that 'The change when the pupil began to read was a change in his *behaviour*; and it makes no sense here to speak of 'a first word in his new state'.' Now he has the interlocutor reply:

> But isn't that only because of our too slight acquaintance with what goes on in the brain and the nervous system? If we had a more accurate knowledge of these things we should see what connexions were established by the training, and then we should be able to say when we looked into his brain: "Now he has *read* this word, now the reading connexion has been set up". – – And [W. now replies] it presumably *must* be like that – for otherwise how could we be so sure that there was such a connexion? That it is so is presumably a priori – or is it only probable? And how probable is it? Now, ask yourself: what do you *know* about these things? – – But if it is a priori, that means that it is a form of account which is very convincing to us. (PI 158)

It looks as though Wittgenstein is here raising a new objection to the idea that reading – and the same goes for understanding – might be a state of somebody's brain. The objection appears to be this: there is no reason to suppose *a priori* that any such state underlies the behaviour characteristic of somebody who can read in Wittgenstein's sense. To put it in the terminology of the preceding sections: there is no reason to suppose that *any* neural B-dispositions underlie the behavioural A-dispositions that interest us, for example, the disposition to convert a written text into the pattern of sounds that we conventionally associate with it.

I said at 3.2.1 that it would be very surprising if we found A-dispositions that were not as it were underwritten by any B-dispositions.[13] But Wittgenstein considered it a real possibility in the psychological sphere. That is, he thought that the behavioural dispositions by whose manifestations the pupil shows that he can read, or has mastered a series, might have *no* explanation in terms of his brain-states. A famous sequence of remarks from his late writings on the philosophy of mind illustrates what alternative he prefers; here are two extracts from it.

No supposition seems to me more natural than that there is no process in the brain correlated with associating or with thinking; so that it would be impossible to read off thought-processes from brain processes. I mean this: if I talk or write there is, I assume, a system of impulses going out from my brain and correlated with my spoken or written thoughts. But why should the system continue further in the direction of the centre? Why should this order not proceed, so to speak, out of chaos? (Z 608)

I saw this man years ago: now I have seen him again, I recognize him, I remember his name. And why does there have to be a cause of this remembering in my nervous system? Why must something or other, whatever it may be, be stored up there *in any form*? Why *must* a trace have been left behind? Why should there not be a psychological regularity to which *no* physiological regularity corresponds? If this upsets our concept of causality then it is high time that it was upset. (Z 610; cf. Z 609, 611–13)

These remarks do nothing to refute the presumption in favour of such a correlation; but what they do make clear is that it is really an empirical matter whether or not any particular 'psychological regularity' corresponds to a physiological one.

Note the difference between *this* objection to the identification of understanding with a state, and the objection at PI 149. The objection of PI 149 – as I am interpreting it here – is that understanding is not a state or B-disposition of the mind or the brain, in fact not a state *at all*, because given one's A-dispositions, whether one understands is of necessity quite independent of one's B-dispositions. This might be true even though one's actual B-dispositions *explained* one's A-dispositions, just as the actual facts about its surface reflectance might explain an object's colour. Whereas the present objection is that there might not *be* any B-dispositions in the brain *to* explain one's A-dispositions: so no brain-state is even a *candidate* for being 'the state of understanding', quite independently of the first objection.

The effectiveness or otherwise of this second objection depends so heavily upon the success and prospects of empirical research into the brain that further comment upon it would be out of place here. I shall only say that the first objection seems to me to be quite effective enough to make this second one otiose.

3.3. Understanding and guidance

3.3.1. A dilemma

At PI 151 Wittgenstein introduces another example. A writes down a series of numbers and B is trying to detect the principle of the series, that is, the rule for any step in the series given all the preceding ones. For instance if A writes down '1, 2, 3, . . .' then the principle of the series is that each element is got by adding 1 to the preceding one. Or if A writes down '1, 4, 9, 16, . . .' then the principle of the series is that for each natural number n, the nth element of the series is the square of n. What interests Wittgenstein is the question of what happens when B suddenly grasps the principle of a series: the example he gives begins '1, 5, 11, 19, 29, . . .'. And the reason for his interest is obvious: this example, like those at PI 139 and PI 141, is a case in which an episode of understanding seems to contain the whole future development of the series (or the whole use of a word) within itself and thereby to *guide* one's use.

Wittgenstein first imagines B experiencing the kind of thing that many people actually observe to be going on when they suddenly understand the principle behind a series. For instance B might simply try out certain formulas until the right one occurs to him. Or he might experience a feeling of tension while 'all sorts of vague thoughts go through his head'. Then he asks himself what the series of differences is; and on seeing that it is '4, 6, 8, 10' he says 'Now I can go on.' Or perhaps he just has a sensation as of a 'light quick intake of breath' and continues the series.

But to which of these types of experience are we referring when we speak of 'the onset of B's understanding'? It looks as though it can't be any of them. For instance, it can't be the occurrence to B of the formula – that is, the appearance in his mind or visibly on paper of the sign '$a_n = n^2 + n - 1$' – because 'it is perfectly imaginable that the formula should occur to him and that he should nevertheless not understand' (PI 152). This form of argument should be familiar from PI 34 (1.2) and PI 139 (3.1.1) and its plausibility is evident. So too is the possibility of generalizing it to cover all of those other experiences that might have occurred when B understood. So it looks as though the onset of B's understanding is *not* a type of experience.

> We are trying to get hold of the mental process of under-standing which seems to be hidden behind those coarser and therefore more readily visible accompaniments. But we do not succeed; or, rather, it does not get as far as a real attempt. For even supposing I had found something that had hap-pened in all those cases of understanding, – why should *it* be the understanding? (PI 153)

But if understanding is not an overt process, neither can it be a covert process. For 'how can the process of understanding have been hidden, when I said "Now I understand" *because* I understood?! And if I say it is hidden – then how do I know what I have to look for?' (ibid., cf. PI 147a).

Wittgenstein has therefore reached an intolerable dilemma. On the one hand there appears to be no special experience of understanding because any such experience could equally accompany misunderstanding. But on the other hand if the onset of understanding does *not* impinge upon my awareness as such, what justifies B's saying that he *does* understand? Surely one *is* often enough justified in saying that, for instance in cases when one *has* understood.

He resolves this tension in the very next section. The statement 'Now I understand' does not describe *any* type of process. So awareness of any such type of process was never going to be sufficient to justify anyone's saying 'Now I understand!' There are instead '*particular circumstances*, which justify me in saying I can go on – when the formula occurs to me' (PI 154).

Now what exactly does this mean? In order to get clear on this point Wittgenstein begins an extended discussion of *reading* in the sense introduced at 3.2.2, and we turn now to this.

3.3.2. *Reading, derivation and guidance*

The discussion of reading at PI 156–78 in fact serves three purposes. One of these is to illustrate in connection with a relatively *simple* psychological verb ('read' as against 'understand') how such terms can fail to denote *any* type of process, conscious or otherwise. The second is to illustrate how one can be none the less *justified* in attributing that expression to oneself, and in particular how it is the *circumstances* of the utterance that can do the justifying.

But a third purpose has to do with the nature and not only the simplicity of reading. It is natural to suppose that when one is reading a text out loud one does not merely utter the words at the same time as looking at the text; rather one's speech is *derived from* or *guided by* the printed letters. This notion of derivation is also a component of the more complex notion of understanding. Someone who thought that the understanding was a sort of 'reservoir from which our acts spring' is going to think that as well as a state of understanding there is an act of *deriving* one's applications, for example, of a word from that state; or an experience of having that state *guide* one's applications of the word. So by arguing that 'derivation' and 'guidance' do not themselves denote any type of process, Wittgenstein will not only have established the same for 'reading'; he will also have further undermined that misconception of understanding itself.

At PI 162 he suggests that we define 'reading' as follows: one reads when one derives the reproduction from the original. Now what *is* this process of derivation? One can certainly give examples of cases that seem clearly enough to involve it. For instance, suppose that we have taught someone a rule for turning a printed text into a handwritten one. To this end we might give him a table consisting of two columns, each row of which matches a printed letter on the left with its cursive equivalent on the right. 'And he shews that he is deriving his script from the printed words by consulting the table' (PI 162).

But it is possible to interpret the table in more than one way. It might happen that instead of matching a printed letter with the cursive equivalent to its right, the pupil matches a printed letter with the cursive one that is one below it and to the right: so he matches *A* with *b*, *C* with *d*, . . . and *Z* with *a* (i.e. in accordance with the second schema drawn at PI 86). Surely he would still count as *deriving* his script from the printed words, although possibly not in the way that we had originally intended. Or it might happen that his method evolves by the rule that if on one day he writes (e.g.) *c* for *B*, then on the next day he writes *d* for *B*, and so on. Or perhaps that he so evolves each time he comes to the same letter, so that if one *B* in a text gets transcribed as *d*, the next one gets transcribed as *e*.

The point of this sequence of examples is that at no point in it do we seem to lose anything that was essential to the *derivation* that was clearly going on in the first case. And yet it is clear that the further along the sequence we go, the more closely the procedures resemble random ones. And we can imagine extending the sequence so that eventually we get procedures that *are* random; and yet no clear dividing line separates the procedures that are random from those that involve derivation (PI 163).

Wittgenstein concludes from this that deriving is a family resemblance concept; so too therefore is reading.

> For certainly [the initial case] was a special case of deriving; what is essential to deriving, however, was not hidden beneath the surface of this case, but this 'surface' was one case out of the family of cases of deriving.
>
> And in the same way we also use the word "to read" for a family of cases. And in different circumstances we apply different criteria for a person's reading. (PI 164)

Now that may all be true but it surely is not what the example showed. The example alluded to a sequence of examples of which the first definitely was a case of derivation and the last definitely was not; the point of it was that each step seemed to have as good a claim to count as an instance of derivation as the preceding one. But this relies not on the *family resemblance* character of the concept 'derive' but on its *vagueness*: for all that it tells us there *may well* be just one feature of 'derivations' that makes us call them that – all it says is that if so then that feature admits of borderline cases.

But even if he *had* shown that what we call 'derivations' form a family, that by itself would not be enough to show that there was no one such type of process (which was one of the claims about understanding that he was trying to illustrate). It would only show that many processes that differed in a variety of *other* ways could all belong to this one type (cf. the discussion of PI 33 on 'attending to the colour' at 1.2).

In fact the example can seem doubly irrelevant. For the other claim about understanding that Wittgenstein may be trying to illustrate is that I am justified in saying that *I* have understood the sequence, not because of any particular kind of experience but because of the particular circumstances in which I say it. But the sequence of examples does not illustrate that point either, because they are all described from a *third*-person perspective: they concern the circumstances in which we are justified in saying that somebody else has derived the script from the text. So even if it is true that *we* are justified, in saying of the pupil that he has derived from the text, by the special circumstances in which we say it, nothing follows as to whether *he* is similarly justified in saying that of himself. For what justifies a third-personal claim might be very different from what justifies the corresponding first-personal one, as Wittgenstein himself emphasizes elsewhere (4.2.5). But Wittgenstein does discuss the first-personal perspective on reading very shortly afterwards, so let us now turn to that.

Are we aware of a difference between a case of genuinely reading a sequence of letters – say the sequence 'A B O V E' – and a case of uttering the sequence while looking at the letters (as a man might do who could speak but not read English)? It seems as though we are – in particular it is tempting to suppose that we are aware not just of the coincidence of our utterance with our seeing of the corresponding letters; we are aware of the latter somehow *guiding* the former (PI 170b), or as Wittgenstein also puts it, a feeling of causal connection (PI 169a) or of influence (PI 169c):

> We imagine that a feeling enables us to perceive as it were a connecting mechanism between the look of the word and the sound that we utter. For when I speak of the experiences of being influenced, of causal connexion, of being guided, that is really meant to imply that I as it were feel the movement of the lever which connects seeing the letters with speaking. (PI 170)

But *do* we have any such feeling?

Against the idea that we have any feeling of causal connection Wittgenstein writes:

> Causation is surely something established by experiments, by observing a regular concomitance of events for example. So how could I say that I *felt* something that is established by experiment? (PI 169)

Without supplementation this argument can easily seem most implausible. The fact that we can establish something by one sort of procedure (an experiment) doesn't exclude its being detected by another ('feeling' it). We can establish that somebody has an upset stomach by performing certain experiments; but he can tell it in another way too – by feeling it. So *of course* we can say that you feel something that may also be established by experiment. Where is the difficulty?[14]

One way to make the argument look more plausible would be to emphasize the point about the *regular* concomitance of events. On a regularity account (and on many other accounts) of what it is, the obtaining of a causal connection has consequences that are spread over time and space, whereas one cannot *feel* something of *that* extent but only how things are with one *here and now*. So one cannot 'feel' the obtaining of a causal connection because it is spread over space and time in a way that the contents of one's feeling cannot be. Of course one can see *some* things and events at distant times and places, for example, stars and sunsets; but that is not the same thing as seeing the whole panoply of correlations (past *and* future) that we are supposing a causal connection between two types of event to involve.

But if that is the argument then it is implausible, if only because it appears to confuse the content of an experience with its cause. And in fact there *is* a sort of experience that can easily seem to be of just such an extended regularity. What I have in mind is this (the example appears at RFM IV-39): if by looking at a token of the word 'Bismarck' one sees that it has eight letters, what one also sees is that that *type* of word has eight letters, that is, that every one of its tokens, past, present and future and wherever they may be, has eight letters. Why does this not count as 'experiencing a regularity?' Similarly then, when one reads a new word out loud, why could it not be part of one's experience that this type of sound goes with that type of printed pattern?

Still, Wittgenstein has a further and better argument against the idea that what justifies one in saying that one was guided is a type of experience that distinguishes the presence of guidance from its absence. Like many of his best arguments it appears to involve phenomenological introspection. It is that when you observe what actually happens in such cases you will notice that there is in fact *no experience at all* that could be 'the experience of guidance':

> Make some arbitrary doodle on a bit of paper – – And now make a copy next to it, let yourself be guided by it. – – I should like to say: "Sure enough, I was guided here. But as for what was characteristic in what happened – if I say what happened, I no longer find it characteristic."
>
> But now notice this: *while* I am being guided everything is quite simple, I notice nothing *special*; but afterwards, when I ask myself what it was that happened, it seems to have been something indescribable. *Afterwards* no description satisfies me. It's as if I couldn't believe that I merely looked, made such-and-such a face, and drew a line. – But don't I *remember* anything else? No . . . (PI 175)

I think we should take this as making an introspective case for the empirical conclusion that no such 'experience of guidance' exists; taken as such it seems to me as decisive as Hume's argument against any special experience of a self (*Treatise* I.iv.6).

It is worth noting that in addition to this rather straightforward point Wittgenstein appears to have a subtler one in mind. He says:

> When I look back on the experience I have the feeling that what is essential about it is an 'experience of being influenced', of a connexion – as opposed to any mere simultaneity of phenomena: but at the same time I should not be willing to call any experienced phenomenon the "experience of being influenced". (This contains the germ of the idea that the will is not a *phenomenon.*) (PI 176)

This argument is not simply a report that he has looked within himself for an 'experience of the because' and come up short, just as one might fail, for example, to find an experience of acidity when tasting wine. It is rather a claim that nothing *could* be that experience.

But why not? In *Philosophical Investigations* he does not say. One reason might be that to 'experience the because' is to experience a regularity, and he might have thought – for the reason already criticized – that nothing could be an experience of a regularity. Another line of thought is this: he had once thought that the content of both experience and linguistic description had to be contingent: 'Whatever we see could be other than it is. Whatever we can describe at all could be other than it is' (TLP 5.634). Now the traditional conception of causation involves *necessary* connection: if an event A is a sufficient cause for another event B then A *could not* have occurred without B. Putting these two ideas together we reach the conclusion that to 'experience the because' is to experience a necessary connection, that is, just the sort of experience that the *Tractatus* had ruled out.

Whether or not it *was* what Wittgenstein had in mind, this line of thought faces the same objection as its predecessor: when you see that the word 'Bismarck' has eight letters, why are you not seeing not only that things *are* but also that they *must* be a certain way, and hence experiencing a necessary connection as well as a regularity? And this is to say nothing of the dubious association between causation and necessary connection. But in any case the straightforward introspective argument appears to me already to have established the point at which PI 176 was aimed – that is, that there *is* no 'experience of guidance' – so I shall leave the matter there.

But if there is no such experience then what was the source of our mistake? Why did we think that there must be one? Wittgenstein's answer at this point sounds rather Kantian. It is as though we impose the concept of guidance upon a stream of sensational input in which it does not originate:

> I should like to say "I experience the because". Not because I remember such an experience, but because when I reflect on what I experience in such a case I look at it through the medium of the concept 'because' (or 'influence' or 'cause' or 'connexion'). (PI 177)

But what does it really mean to look at something 'through the medium of the concept'?

Here Wittgenstein does not say; but I think that what he means is not at all Kantian. Instead, 'looking at it through the medium of the concept' means: failing to reflect that 'guidance'—which he runs together with 'influence' and other such words at PI 175b—expresses a family resemblance concept. If one thinks that there must be some one thing that makes us apply the concept 'guidance' in all the cases where we do apply it, then of course one is bound to postulate a typical experience of guidance even if most of the time you do not remember one. Wittgenstein's discussion is aimed at loosening the grip of that preconception: thus in addition to the direct argument just cited he gives a list of various activities that count as guidance (PI 172). The upshot is supposed to be that not only do we no longer take guidance to be a unitary kind of mental experience at all; but also, we are free of the conceptual prejudice that had attracted us to that view, as it were in spite of ourselves.

But then if it does not describe anything you experience, what *does* justify an assertion that one is reading, that one has derived the script from the printed text, or that one understands the principle behind the series? Wittgenstein doesn't – although he very well could – use the example of guidance to illustrate the point. Instead he returns to the example that PI 151 introduced. Recall that A writes down a series of numbers and B is trying to detect the principle of the series, that is, the rule for any step in the series given all the preceding ones. For example, if A writes down '1, 2, 3, . . .' then the principle of the series is that each element is got by adding 1 to the preceding element. What justifies B in saying 'Now I understand'? Here is the answer:

> It is clear that we should not say B has the right to say the words "Now I know how to go on", just because he thought of the formula – unless experience shewed that there was a connexion between thinking of the formula – saying it, writing it down – and actually continuing the series. And obviously such a connexion does exist. (PI 179)

What 'experience shews' is not some *necessary* connection but only a statistical association. It is because of *our* experience that most of the time, when B – or somebody like him – has the 'thinking of the formula' experience,[15] he continues the series correctly, we are right to call B justified in saying that he knows how to go on.

Now to say what justifies an assertion is not to say what it describes, and Wittgenstein immediately blocks that interpretation of him. In particular then, he denies that 'Now I understand' is B's way of saying 'Now I am having an experience that I know empirically to lead to the continuation of the series.' For as we saw in connection with 'guidance', B might be justified in saying 'Now I know how to go on' even if nothing at all occurs in his mind (PI 179c). And it would be quite misleading to call B's words in *that* case a description of either a mental state or anything else. 'One might rather call them a "signal"; and we judge whether it was rightly employed by what he goes on to do' (PI 180).

Nor, from B's own point of view, is his assertion 'Now I know how to go on' or 'Now I understand' in any sense *derived from* or otherwise supported by his awareness that he can usually continue the series in circumstances in which he typically says that. For one doesn't argue like this: 'I have always been able to continue the series when the formula has occurred to me in the past, so it will happen now too.' If anything, an experience such as the occurrence of the formula to B is the *cause* and not the *ground* of his certainty that he can continue the series (PI 325).

We might illustrate the point with the following analogy. A dog that has repeatedly got its dinner upon the sounding of a bell, and only then, will soon acquire the habit of salivating whenever it hears one. We might call the salivation 'justified', not because it *describes* an empirical regularity connecting the bell and the dinner, or even because the *dog* knows but cannot speak of such a regularity – it may show no other signs of expecting dinner – but simply because the regularity *exists*. Similarly, it is an extremely general fact of nature that when B and people like him say 'Now I understand the series', they are in fact able to continue the series; and it is the existence of this regularity – whether or not B believes in it – that justifies B.

But then B may not be able to cite any reason for saying that he can continue the series: so *is* he really *justified* in saying that he understands? I think Wittgenstein would regard that question as one of those cases in which ordinary language goes on philosophical holiday (PI 38). On the ordinary sense, that is, the ordinary use of the word 'justified', B *is* justified. 'A good ground is one that looks *like this*' (PI 486). I shall return to this point at 3.4.3.

The feeling can persist that when one's understanding of the series makes its first appearance, it isn't something that just *happens typically* to precede its successful development, that is, as a matter of empirical fact. Instead the whole series seems contained within one's momentary understanding in some other and more instantaneous way. The same feeling arises when we contemplate the giving of an order, say, to continue a series: it is as though the whole series were somehow contained within that order, or whatever lay behind it, in a more intimate way than simply its being *typically* associated with some and not other patterns of behaviour. After all, one can order someone to continue a particular series, and to mean *that very* series, *whether or not* he then carries it out.

'We are – as it were – surprised, not at anyone's knowing the future, but at his being able to prophesy at all (right or wrong). As if the mere prophecy, no matter whether true or false, foreshadowed the future . . .' (PI 461). It is the attempt to get clear on this 'foreshadowing' that ushers in the most celebrated and controversial material in the book.

3.4. The paradox

3.4.1. The possibility of deviance

Let us return to the example of PI 143 (introduced at the start of 3.2) and imagine that the pupil has mastered the series of natural numbers. And let us now write '+n' for the series

'0, n, 2n, . . .', so that '+2' abbreviates the series '0, 2, 4, 6, . . .' and '+3' abbreviates the series '0, 3, 6, 9, . . .'. And suppose that the pupil appears to understand the series +2 perfectly well because he has passed all our tests of his ability to write down initial segments of it. Suppose finally that in these tests the pupil was never (as it happens) asked to extend the series +2 (or any other series) beyond 1000.

Now we ask him to continue the series +2 beyond 1000 and, instead of '1000, 1002, 1004, 1006' he writes '1000, 1004, 1008, 1012'. Then we shall say that he has got the series wrong. Moreover, what he has done is to write down something contrary to what we meant *when* we gave the order. And now it looks as though, for that to be the case, we shall have to say that there was something going on *when* we meant it that anticipated *all* of the elements of +2 beyond 1000, not only 1002, 1004, 1006, but also 1866, 1868, 1870 and countless others that equally never occurred to us at the time of giving the order.

But there may have been nothing in the order – or in our minds at the time – that could possibly have shown him that. If we say, 'You were meant to add two: look how you began the series!' he may reply, 'Yes, isn't it right? I thought that was how I was meant to do it!'; if we say, 'You are supposed to do the same thing at every stage!' he may reply, 'Yes, wasn't I doing the same thing?'; if we show him a table correlating each step with the number to be written at that step, he may read it in some deviant manner (cf. those at PI 86, PI 163) that legitimates his own practice; and if we supplement the table with arrows, he may so interpret *them* as to do the same. 'Here it looks as if the order were beginning to stammer. As if the signs were precariously trying to evoke understanding in [him]' (PI 433).

The point can now be made very general. *Any* stage of the series +2 – or of any other sequence – that he has not encountered before might be the starting-point for some deviance on the part of a perfectly rational man who has received exactly the same training as those from whose continuation he is deviating. Thus there might be a pupil who began the series +3 '0, 3, 9, . . .' but on passing 57 wrote '66, 75, 84', that is, appending the continuation of what *we* should call the series +9.

And there is no reason to restrict the point to numerical sequences. A similar deviancy might enter into *any* novel application by a rational person of *any* word: there might, for example, be a rational person who has been trained as we have in the use of the word 'cube' and who has so far applied it in just the way that we should expect, but who now applies it not to newly encountered cubes but to newly encountered triangular prisms.

Finally, there is no reason for the deviancy to begin with a *novel* application: somebody might use the word 'green' for green objects that he has observed hitherto and blue ones that he observes from now on, including those that he has already seen and classified. (He will say that they have 'turned green' if they were blue all along; he will say that they have 'remained green' if they have changed from green to blue between what *we* should call the two classificatory eras.) In short, for *any* application of *any* word, a man who has been trained just as we have been trained might dispute this application with us, however obvious it may seem; and there need be nothing we can point to in our common prior training or in the word's agreed prior use – or in anything else of which we are both aware – to which he will acknowledge that his 'deviant' application is unfaithful.

This means that we were wrong after all to suppose that the rule or order contains its future applications in some special way; that is, in some way of which the 'merely' statistical connection described at PI 179 falls short. For if it did, then we ought to be able to point to something in it that would convince any deviant of his error. But there is nothing in it that might do that: given anything that was going on at the time of giving the order, we can imagine a rational pupil being perfectly aware of it and yet persisting in his deviance.

Similarly neither a sign nor any mental accompaniment of it carries within itself the particular meaning that it seems to intimate to *us*. Rather, what makes it a sign of *this* rather than *that* is how we normally respond to it. That is what justifies my responding to it in one way rather than another on *this* occasion.

Let me ask this: what has the expression of a rule – say a sign-post – got to do with my actions? What sort of connexion is there here? – Well, perhaps this one: I have been trained to react to this sign in a particular way, and now I do so react to it.

But that is only to give a causal connexion; to tell how it has come about that we now go by the sign-post; not what this going-by-the-sign really consists in. On the contrary; I have further indicated that a person goes by a sign-post only in so far as there exists a regular use of sign-posts, a custom. (PI 198)

Wittgenstein's treatment of these examples thus uproots the deep and important misconception that meaning and understanding are mental states or occurrences that somehow contain within themselves some particular pattern of usage. But it has seemed to some that Wittgenstein had intended these examples to point at something even more radical: namely, that understanding and meaning are *themselves* an illusion. I turn now to this reading.

3.4.2. Meaning-facts
The possibility, that a rational deviant of the sort described might yet have missed nothing of what went on when we gave the order +2, raises the question: how then did *the person who gave the order* manage to mean the sequence +2 rather than anything else? Indeed when he – or you, or I – develops any sequence, or for that matter obeys any rule at all, in what sense can we be credited with *fidelity* to what we meant all along? Shouldn't we rather compare the announcement of a rule – say, the formula of a series – with the first stroke of paint on a blank canvas? That is, it is an illusion to suppose that any rule for their use, or indeed any prior use at all, *ever* distinguishes correct from incorrect patterns of use – of words or of anything else. We still have to choose at every stage whether to continue the pattern in one way or another.

Wittgenstein can certainly seem to be denying that a rule ever *can* lay down an application in this way. On the contrast between thinking of understanding as a kind of insight and thinking of it as a kind of choice, he writes:

"What you are saying, then, comes to this: a new insight – intuition – is needed at every step to carry out the order '+n' correctly." – To carry it out correctly! How is it decided what is the right step to take at any particular stage? . . . It would

almost be more correct to say, not that an intuition was
needed at every stage, but that a new decision was needed at
every stage. (PI 186)

And shortly afterwards he makes explicit the general form of the
problem that provoked this talk of 'decision':

But how [the interlocutor asks] can a rule shew me what
I have to do at *this* point? Whatever I do is, on some interpretation, in accord with the rule. (PI 198)

This is the famous 'rule-following' paradox that dominates
Kripke's notorious reading of Wittgenstein.

Kripke's account of the paradox is not a thesis about what
Wittgenstein actually meant; instead it presents thoughts that
Wittgenstein's argument provoked in Kripke (Kripke 1982: 5).
But (quite apart from its intrinsic interest) it is still worth
examining in order clearly to distinguish Wittgenstein's own
line from it.

According to Kripke (pp. 9, 21) the considerations that I have
just mentioned (about deviant usage) give rise to a question that
I shall put in terms of Wittgenstein's example, not his: what fact
was there about me, at the time of giving the order to continue
the sequence +2 beyond 1000, in virtue of which I meant all
along that its recipient was to write, say, 1868 after 1866, or
10004 after 10002 (or any other pair that I did not explicitly
mention at the time of giving the order)? In the course of a very
penetrating discussion Kripke examines and rejects certain
candidate facts: facts about my verbal training (pp. 15–16), facts
about my dispositions to respond in one way or another
(pp. 22–37), facts about the relative simplicity of the competing
interpretations (pp. 38–9), facts about my introspectible mental
state (pp. 41–50) and *sui generis* facts about my mind (pp. 51–4).
He concludes that there is *no* such fact. Therefore a rule cannot
tell me what to do, and there is no such thing as meaning anything by a rule. That is Kripke's interpretation of the following
celebrated passage:

This was our paradox: no course of action could be determined
by a rule, because any course of action can be made out to

accord with the rule. The answer was: if *any* action can be made out to accord with the rule, then it can also be made out to conflict with it. And so there would be neither accord nor conflict here. (PI 201)

Kripke takes this to be Wittgenstein's conclusion and he draws the obvious and dramatic corollary. 'There can be no such thing as meaning anything by any word. Each new application we make is a leap in the dark; any present intention could be interpreted so as to accord with anything we may choose to do. So there can be neither accord, nor conflict' (p. 55).

Hence we do not speak of any *facts* when we say, for example: 'You meant the series +2 when you ordered the pupil to write down the series.' But according to Kripke, that does not mean that we should drop such talk altogether. Rather, we should note that even if a sentence like that describes no facts, it can still possess *assertibility* conditions. These are rules defeasibly licensing its assertion under certain conditions. Those conditions are essentially comparative: you are (defeasibly) licensed to assert, for example, 'Jones means addition by his sign "+"' if *his* use of that sign – in the cases where he has applied it – matches *your* use of '+' or 'addition' (pp. 89–90). Talk about meaning is therefore based essentially on a comparison in a way that inverts common-sense. It is not that you and Jones both use '+' in the same way because you have both attached the same meaning to it; rather, we are entitled to say that you have attached the same meaning to '+' *if* you both use it in roughly the same way. It is in this essentially comparative dimension of meaning-attributions that Kripke locates the kernel of Wittgenstein's private language argument (pp. 87–113).

Before assessing this interpretation of Wittgenstein it is worth mentioning that it offers us a deeper account of his response to the difficulties concerning vagueness that I mentioned at 2.2.3 (a) (ii). Recall the difficulty: the rules governing our use of vague predicates may well make it possible to construct a finite sequence of objects in such a way that some such predicate definitely applies to the first and not to the last object in the sequence, while simultaneously insisting that one apply the predicate to an object if and only if one applies it to whatever lies next to it in the sequence. This would show the rules to be inconsistent; and the pragmatic attitude that I there attributed to Wittgenstein was that this does not make the concept unusable so long as our use of the rules never in fact confronts us with a contradiction. Kripke's interpretation reveals the possibility of a different response. For if the rules 'for using a predicate' in fact do not determine any one pattern of use rather than any other, then until we actually find a real Sorites sequence and by making successive applications of the rules arrive at the contradiction, that contradiction is *not even implicit* in those rules. Thus the rules governing a vague predicate would be as harmless as – because as impotent as – those governing any other expression.

Turning back to Kripke, I think it is fairly certain that Wittgenstein is not arguing in the way that Kripke presents him. One fairly clear indication of this is the remark at PI 136a: if as it says ' "p" is true' is just another way to say 'p', then so is ' "p" expresses a *fact*' or 'It is a *fact* that p'. But then the propriety of 'He meant +2' stands or falls with that of 'It is a *fact* that he meant +2'; and so once we are entitled to say the former – even if only in accordance with Kripke's own 'assertibility conditions' – there is simply no room for denying the latter. In short Wittgenstein's own theory of truth commits him to rejecting any sort of distinction of the sort that Kripke wants to draw, between those assertoric sentences that really do, and those that only seem to, state the facts.[16]

Note in addition that according to Kripke's reading there is *no* conflict between what occurs to one when one 'understands' a word and whatever one then goes on to do with it. But Wittgenstein denies just this. Recall his discussion of the idea that what comes before one's mind when one understands a word is a picture. He writes: 'Can there be a collision between picture and application? There can . . .' (PI 141c). Or again:

"But I already knew, at the time when I gave the order, that he ought to write 1002 after 1000." – Certainly; and you can also say you *meant* it then . . . (PI 187)

So certainly Wittgenstein, unlike Kripke, does *not* deny that you mean or intend one thing and not another when you state a rule; nor does he deny that the auditor's action – his application of a word, for instance, or his continuation of a sequence – can accord with what was meant, or that it can *conflict* with what was meant. And as we have seen, what justifies our saying – or your saying – that you meant one thing rather than another, is the customary *use* of the expression.

3.4.3. *'Something animal'*

This line of thought faces an objection that may be introduced by means of the second paragraph of PI 201, where Wittgenstein replies to Kripkean scepticism about the possibility of meaning *anything*:

> It can be seen that there is a misunderstanding here from the mere fact that in the course of our argument we give one interpretation after another; as if each one contented us at least for a moment, until we thought of yet another standing behind it. What this shews is that there is a way of grasping a rule which is *not* an *interpretation*, but which is exhibited in what we call "obeying the rule" and "going against it" in actual cases.

What he means by 'giving one interpretation after another' is different descriptions of ways that one could take the rule: so, for instance, one interpretation of '+2' would be 'Add 2 to each number in the sequence to get the next one.' Another interpretation of it would be 'Add 2 to each number less than 1000 to get the next one. Add 4 to each number greater than or equal to 1000 to get the next one.' And of course we can think of indefinitely many others. (Do not confuse this use of 'interpretation' with that at PI 34.)

But the fact that we can think of all these interpretations does *not* show that we never understood the rule in one way rather than another, or that it never tells us what to do. The rule does tell us what to do, because there is a way that we do in fact respond to the rule. In general we *do in fact* respond to the rule by adding 2 to each number to get the next one; we do in fact say that somebody who responds otherwise is 'going against it', and so on; and *that is why* the rule tells us to do that and not something else.

It is important to be clear about what Wittgenstein does mean, and what he does not mean, by 'what we call "obeying the rule" and "going against it" in actual cases.' He is *not* saying that what you mean by a rule on an occasion is altogether settled by what *you* call 'obeying the rule', or by what the intended auditor calls that, in *this* case – on the first alternative it would be possible to mean '+2' by 'bububu' (a nonsense expression, cf. PI p. 16n/18n); on the second alternative it would be *im*possible ever to go *against* a rule.

What he is saying is rather that what exhibits one's grasp of a rule is what is *generally* called 'obeying the rule' and 'going against it', that is, by *myself* at other times or by *other* people, possibly at the same time, but in any case in ordinary circumstances. Suppose that by my utterance of '+2' I meant that he ought to write, for example, '1868' after '1866' but that nothing in my inner or outer behaviour, or in his, settled this. (I never mentioned those numbers, and I never thought of them, and neither did he.) Then what exhibits the fact that I did mean him to write '1868' after '1866' is the fact that *other* people *have* continued the series in that way. It is an instance of what they call 'obeying the rule'; just as writing, say, '1870' immediately after '1866' is an instance of what they call 'going against it'; and they do so in ordinary circumstances, for instance, in the classroom.

You will immediately object that when I said '+2' I meant: not only certain segments of the sequence that have not occurred to me but which have occurred to others. I also meant segments of the sequence that never *have* occurred to me or to anyone else. For instance, when I said '+2' I meant that he should write 10004 after 10002, but even if nobody had ever written down or thought of those numbers I should still have meant just what I actually did mean; and so I should even in that situation have meant that he should write 10004 after 10002. So how can 'what we call "obeying the rule" and "going against it" in actual cases' exhibit my having meant just that by '+2'?

The answer is that you can *exhibit* something that points beyond the examples that you explicitly mention or that anyone has ever mentioned. We can do this by the use of 'and so on' or ellipsis (PI 208g, NB 49). Teaching by example may also be an exhibition of that sort. For instance, if I wish to explain the word 'game' to somebody I may describe a few games and then I might add 'This *and similar things* are called games' (PI 69). Here the

expression 'and similar things' is performing the function that
might in the explanation of other words have been performed by
'and so on' or by '. . .'. Or again I may explain the word 'same' to
someone by example.

> In the course of this teaching I shall shew him the same
> colours, the same lengths, the same shapes, I shall make
> him find them and produce them, and so on. I shall,
> for instance, get him to continue an ornamental pattern
> uniformly when told to do so. – And also to continue pro-
> gressions. And so, for example, when given: . .. ... to go
> on: .... (PI 208)

As well as being one itself this passage describes two further
'exhibitions of meaning' by example: one exhibits what one
means by 'same' by showing the pupil examples of 'same F';
and then *he* exhibits what he has understood by giving *other*
examples. It is in this and similar ways, then, that one's meaning
may be 'exhibited in what we call "obeying the rule" and "going
against it" in actual cases'.

But mustn't this 'exhibition' of what you meant still miss out
on something? Let us suppose that up to this point nobody has
ever concerned themselves with what number follows '1866' in
the sequence +2. But when you gave the order '+2' you certainly
meant that the pupil should write '1868' after '1866'. Wittgenstein
says that that is what our judgement about actual cases
'exhibits'; this is exhibited to me, or to a competent pupil, not
by your having mentioned *that particular example*, but by your
having mentioned other examples: say, by your having written
'998' after '996', or by your having written '212' after '210', and
so on. But the complaint is: how can you have exhibited that
you meant *just that* by your talk of *other* examples? As the
interlocutor puts it: '[D]o you really explain to the other person
what you yourself understand? Don't you get him to *guess* the
essential thing? You give him examples, – but he has to guess
their drift, to guess your intention' (PI 210).

The answer to this objection is first of all to expand it. For if
it applies at all it does not only apply in cases where the sequence
that one is supposed to have in mind reaches beyond all of the
segments of it that one has actually mentioned, written down or

otherwise made explicit (if only to oneself).[17] Suppose, for instance, that you did somehow write down in a legible fashion the entirety of the sequence +2, so that nobody who read it could be in any doubt that you had '1868' after '1866'. Your pupil would still be in as much need of guesswork as before. For he would still have just as much need to guess at the 'method of projection' from your script to his: what transformation is to count as writing down the *same* as what you have written down – is it the numbers that you have written down, or what you get by adding 0 to the first, 2 to the second, 4 to the third . . .?

That is wrong; where we have gone wrong is through applying an absurdly severe conception of what 'exhibiting one's meaning' involves. What the objector is insisting upon is that in order to exhibit that I mean one thing I must eliminate *all possible alternatives* because my hearer is otherwise reduced to guessing between the uneliminated ones. But according to Wittgenstein it is not really *guessing* to which one is reduced. The passage just quoted from PI 210 continues:

> Any explanation which I can give myself I give to him too. –
> "He guesses what I intend" would mean: various interpretations of my explanation come to his mind, and he lights on one of them. So in this case he could ask; and I could and should answer him.

Here 'interpretration' presumably has the sense recommended for it at PI 201, that is, 'the substitution of one expression of the rule for another'. So to say that somebody guesses what you meant means that various alternative descriptions of rules that you might mean actually occur to him. Even if indefinitely many continuations are compatible with the examples that you have shown him (as will always be the case), he is *not* guessing *unless* a number of them occur to him and he chooses from among them. So if in fact no interpretation occurs to him, if instead he merely continues the sequence as you wished, then he has *not* had to guess.

Now this sense of 'guess' almost certainly preserves something that belongs to the everyday use of the word 'guess' but which the interlocutor's more 'philosophical' usage in PI 210 appears to have discarded: namely, the intuition that when in ordinary cases the pupil learns by example, he is *not* guessing. In this case our language has gone on what Wittgenstein would call a holiday (PI 38). We feel as thought we had made the exciting discovery that one can only ever *guess* at another's meaning. But that is not an everyday use of the word 'guess'.

But although unfaithful to the intuitive extension of the word 'guess', the interlocutor's use of it at PI 210 does legitimately highlight something in its intuitive *intension*. This is the idea that one is guessing if one does not reach one's conclusion *through a rational process*. And it *is* reasonable to describe many learning situations as being of that sort. For instance, suppose again that the pupil is asked to continue the sequence +2 in the circumstance that nobody has ever developed it past 1866. Then what explains his now writing '1868' rather than, for example, '1870' after '1866'? He cannot point to any reason; or rather, if he points to his teaching and the order itself as a reason, he will not be able to say why he takes that teaching *as* a reason for writing '1868' rather than as a reason for writing '1870'.

Now nothing is gained by insisting that that the pupil is or that he is not 'guessing' in such cases. What matters is what Wittgenstein agrees upon: that we do eventually run up against this giving out of reasons. And he seeks – quite rightly – to downplay its practical significance.

> How can he *know* how he is to continue a pattern by himself – whatever instruction you give him? – Well, how do I know? – – If that means "Have I reasons?" the answer is: my reasons will soon give out. And then I shall act, without reasons. (PI 211)

> When someone whom I am afraid of orders me to continue the series, I act quickly, with perfect certainty, and the lack of reasons does not trouble me. (PI 212)

Now it is certainly possible to overreact to this point, that the pupil does not have a reason for supposing you to mean that he should write, for example, '1868' after '1866'. The overreaction would be to think that we ought always to *doubt* or *hesitate over* any continuation of any order simply because we lack the slightest justification for one continuation rather than another. But that is wrong: the *absence* of any reason for doing A rather than B, and vice versa, is not in itself a reason for *not* doing either. 'To use a word [or continue a pattern] without a justification does not mean to use it without right' (PI 289). Nor do we *in fact* have any doubts, at least not most of the time, for it is not the case 'that we are in doubt because it is possible for us to *imagine* a doubt' (PI 84).[18]

But behind that relatively complacent practical point lies a more unsettling truth about human nature. For if the drift of PI 210–12 is correct then it seems that my understanding of somebody else is better described as animal or instinctive response than as rational. The fact is that the pupil, and other English speakers, just *are* inclined to continue the order '+2' by writing 1868 after 1866, and to regard any other continuation as wrong.

> If I have exhausted the justifications I have reached bedrock, and my spade is turned. Then I am inclined to say: "This is simply what I do." (PI 217)

> When I obey a rule, I do not choose. I obey the rule *blindly*. (PI 219)

What is especially disturbing about this position is that it appears to introduce an element of instinct into what had seemed to be a paradigm of rationality: the continuation of a mathematical sequence. That is not for a moment to impugn the confidence that we rest in such continuations, but only to point out that it arises not from any sort of rational *apprehension* but rather *is* a matter of blind behaviour.

> I want to conceive it as something that lies beyond being justified or unjustified; as it were, as something animal. (OC 359)

Naturalism is the philosophy that sees us as just one animal among others rather than as beings that *reason* has endowed with a special sort of insight; it is an important and general truth that has ethical and political as well as metaphysical implications. Wittgenstein's greatest achievement in *Philosophical Investigations* was to show just how deeply it reaches.

SECTION 4. PRIVACY

What follows the treatment of rule-following, meaning and understanding in *Philosophical Investigations* is an equally subtle and searching discussion of sensations and sensational language.

Part of the interest of that topic arises from the fact that sensational states and processes – toothaches, afterimages, kinaesthetic sensations etc. – have long presented a range of problems to traditional philosophy. Are they identical with physical states and processes or otherwise reducible to them? How can anyone know that anyone else has sensations at all? And even if he knows that, how can he know that anyone else's sensations are *like* his own? For that matter, what explains the special certainty with which he judges his *own* sensations? What *is* it to 'own' a sensation? Wittgenstein does not directly address all of these questions. But he does give us reasons for doubting the reality of the problems that they appear to express.

Another part of its interest lies in the fact that many philosophers have placed sensations at the foundation of language. For instance, we have seen that Locke took words primarily to stand for one's private 'ideas', and one plausible interpretation of 'idea' in this context is 'sensory image'. Indeed we saw that that thought of Locke's was what lay behind an objection (still unanswered) to what seemed to follow from the 'shopping trip' example at PI 1 (1.1). For one might have insisted that the example did not establish any very great diversity among the uses of the words 'five', 'red' and 'apples', on the grounds that if we broaden our view of this example to consider the role that inner states play in it, we see a greater *uniformity* in their uses than superficial consideration could reveal. Also in Wittgenstein's own time the logical positivists had thought that one could (Carnap 2003: s61) or must (Ayer 1971: ch. 2) analyse meaningful statements into statements about one's immediate sensory states.

For sensational states to play the role that they are supposed by these philosophers to have it must be possible for their owners to speak of them without any knowledge of the external or bodily criteria on which their *third*-personal attributions normally rely; indeed this must be possible whether or not they *have* such criteria. A language in which its owner refers to sensations that lack all such criteria is known in the literature as a *private language*;

and we shall look first at two arguments that Wittgenstein presents against its possibility.

Finally, it looks as though private sensational states are a counterexample to some of Wittgenstein's own remarks on meaning and understanding. We have already seen that there need be nothing going on in your awareness at the time, for example, of the picture of a cube's occurring to you that will rule out *some* unintended interpretation of 'cube'; that occurrence does not therefore *force* a particular use upon you (PI 140). Rather, the fact that pictures of cubes customarily have these and not those other uses is what justifies our calling this event the occurrence before your mind of an application (PI 141c; cf. PI 179, 198).

But consider the case of an inner sensory state. Suppose that on some occasion I decide to use a word 'S' to denote sensations of the same type as *this* one – and here I focus on some particular sensation, say my experience of a particular shade of red that I have just noticed. By doing so, it seems that I could (at least in principle) set up an association between the word 'S' and that very shade, so that it is the image of that shade that occurs to me when I say 'S?' to myself. Now couldn't that be a case in which a certain conscious occurrence – what we might call a 'private ostensive definition' – *has* 'forced a use' upon me? Perhaps indeed that is how our actual colour-words get their meaning. 'How is he to know what colour he is to pick out when he hears "red"? – Quite simple: he is to take the colour whose image occurs to him when he hears the word' (PI 239).

So the private ostensive definition appears to put the application of a word before your mind quite independently of any other regularities in the use of the image on which you are then focusing your attention. The first argument that we shall consider is directed against the possibility of such a definition.

4.1. Private language

4.1.1. Preliminaries

Wittgenstein first states his target in the following passage:

A human being can encourage himself, give himself orders, obey, blame and punish himself; he can ask himself a question and answer it. We could even imagine human beings who spoke only in monologue . . .

But could we also imagine a language in which a person could write down or give vocal expression to his inner experiences – his feelings, moods, and the rest – for his private use? . . . The individual words of this language are to refer to what can only be known to the person speaking; to his immediate private sensations. So another person cannot understand the language. (PI 243)

The passage actually appears to confuse two quite different features that languages might have and which would justify the title of 'privacy'; only one of these is of interest to us. In particular, the penultimate sentence says that the words of this language (a) *refer to what can only be known to* its speaker. And the last sentence says that those words (b) *can only be understood by* that speaker. And not only this but also that feature (b) is a consequence of feature (a). Let us call a language with feature (a) *epistemically privileged*; let us call a language with feature (b) *idiolectic*.

Edward Craig has shown quite convincingly (Craig 1997) that a language may be epistemically privileged without being idiolectic (so Wittgenstein's final 'so' is out of place). Consider that for someone else to understand an epistemically privileged language it suffices for him to have a *true belief* about the meanings of its words: knowledge is not necessary. Imagine that Bobby uses 'apple' to denote apples whereas his brother Johnny, whose voice is identical, speaks a variant of English in which 'apple' denotes tomatoes. One of them rings me up and without saying his name asks me to fetch him 'five red apples'. Then he hangs up. I don't know whether the token of 'apples' that I heard on the telephone refers to apples or to tomatoes; still, I guess that it refers to apples, and as it happens I am right. In that case it would be correct to say that I, who did not *know* what my interlocutor meant, had understood the instruction. It would also be correct to say that the person who was giving it to me had successfully communicated with me on that occasion.

In general then, one might understand someone's words without *knowing* what they mean; it is therefore hard to see why any epistemically privileged language must also be idiolectic. And this is also true of the special case at hand: if, for example, I do not and perhaps cannot know whether your word 'red' refers to what I call 'blue' (cf. the famous Lockean fantasy: *Essay* II.xxxii.15) it will suffice for communication between us that I *guess* right. In the case at hand therefore, the two criteria come apart – at any rate, epistemic privilege does not entail idiolect.

Now Wittgenstein later gives a third characterization of his target: he states that what concerns him is a language whose terms refer to states or events that have no natural external (i.e. behavioural or otherwise bodily) signs by which others may judge of their occurrence. That is what he states just before the first argument that I am going to examine (PI 256). For instance, *pins and needles* would not qualify as a referent of a term in a private language if it has characteristic causes (e.g. sitting in one place for a long time); nausea would not qualify if it has characteristic effects (e.g. vomiting); and *toothache* would not qualify because it has characteristic causes (e.g. a rotten tooth) *and* characteristic effects (e.g. clutching one's jaw).

If on the other hand you thought, as a Lockean should[19], that we could not judge of somebody's pins and needles, nausea, and so on by these outer signs, then you *would* allow terms referring to pins and needles, nausea and toothache among those of Wittgenstein's target language, on this third characterization. And you would presumably also hold that English, or a sector of it, was a private language in this third sense, containing as it does terms for pins and needles, nausea and toothache. So an argument against this third sort of language would also be an argument against a Lockean interpretation of English.

Three different kinds of language might therefore count as Wittgenstein's target: (a) A language whose terms refer to items known only to its speaker; (b) A language whose terms can only be understood by its speaker; (c) A language whose terms refer to sensational states and processes that have no external manifestations by which anyone other than their possessor can judge of their occurrence. I shall take Wittgenstein to be arguing against a language of type (c) on the grounds that this makes for the most interesting interpretations of what he says.

4.1.2. 'S' in the diary

One can gather the gist of the first argument from PI 258, which runs as follows:

> Let us imagine the following case. I want to keep a diary about the recurrence of a certain sensation. To this end I associate it with the sign "S" and write this sign in a calendar for every day on which I have the sensation. – – I first want to remark that a definition of the sign cannot be formulated. – But still I can give myself a kind of ostensive definition. – How? Can I point to the sensation? Not in the ordinary sense. But I speak, or write the sign down, and at the same time I concentrate my attention on the sensation – and so, as it were, point to it inwardly. – But what is this ceremony for? for that is all it seems to be! A definition surely serves to establish the meaning of a sign. – Well, that is done precisely by the concentration of my attention; for in this way I impress on myself the connexion between the sign and the sensation. – But "I impress it on myself" can only mean: this process brings it about that I remember the connexion *right* in the future. But in the present case I have no criterion of correctness. One would like to say: whatever is going to seem right to me is right. And that only means that here we can't talk about 'right'.

Although the detailed interpretation of this passage is a matter of some controversy, it is possible to be fairly definite as to its aim and drift.

The quoted section does not make it explicit, but it is clear from the preceding ones that Wittgenstein is here attacking the idea that one can by ostensive definition establish the terms of what I am calling a *private* language. That is, 'S' is supposed to refer to a sensation that has no natural external expression.[20] The aim of the section is then to show that one cannot *establish* the meaning – that is, the reference – of the signs of a private language by means of a private ostensive definition. To show this would perhaps not show that a private language was impossible, but it would make it difficult to see how anyone could learn its terms: difficult, therefore, to accept the Lockean view that natural languages like English have a private sector. It would also be to refute the supposed counterexample that I mentioned at the end of this chapter's introduction. Private ostensive definition was supposed to be a means of presenting the application of a word to its user quite independently of any regularities in the use of the associated image; as such it would be a counterexample to Wittgenstein's doctrine that the way something is meant on an occasion depends on its customary usage. If successful the argument that we are now considering would show that the private ostensive definition would not after all endow the word 'S' with any meaning at all.

The broad drift of the argument is also clear and may be set out as follows. The private diarist wishes to introduce a word 'S' for the type of sensation that he is presently having. And he tries to do it by ostensive definition. But ostensive definition is not just a matter of uttering the defined expression 'S' in the presence of the type of sensation that you are intending to name. Nor is it enough to utter 'S' while *concentrating your attention* on that type. What is needed in addition is that the definition brings it about that the diarist remembers the connection right – the connection, that is, 'between sign and sensation'. But a private ostensive definition cannot bring that about because it supplies no criterion of correctness for my use of 'S'. So the supposed private ostensive definition was not really a definition of 'S' at all. It was an idle ceremony.

But we cannot assess whether the argument thus outlined achieves its aim without examining its details. And with respect to these there is scope for great variety of interpretation. Settling which of these interpretations is the one that Wittgenstein really had in mind would be beyond the scope of this book, even if I were able to do it. So instead I shall simply present the three main interpretations of the argument and say something about their plausibility as arguments.

Consideration of the details of PI 258 naturally gives rise to the following five questions:

(a) What is it to 'remember the connection right'?
(b) Why must a successful ostensive definition bring it about that you remember the connection right?
(c) What is a 'criterion of correctness'?

(d) Why must a successful definition supply a criterion of correctness?

(e) Why does a private ostensive definition fail to meet condition (b) and/or condition (d)?

The three interpretations that I shall consider may be characterized roughly as follows: (i) verificationism – if you name a type 'S' you have to specify evidence for its recurrence, and the private linguist cannot do this; (ii) the meaning-check – if you name a type 'S' then you have to specify a way of checking later *what you meant by it all along*, and the private linguist cannot do this; (iii) sortalism – if you name a type 'S' then you have to specify *what* type of thing you are naming 'S', and the private linguist cannot do this. Let us now consider these three interpretations in turn.

(i) *Verificationism.* According to this interpretation of PI 258 the answers to our questions (a)–(e) may be stated as follows. (a) To 'remember the connection right' is to write 'S' in one's diary for just those days on which the diarist experiences a sensation of the type that he initially named 'S'. (b) A successful ostensive definition must bring this about because if one uses 'S' in some very different way then it has not established a connection between sign and sensation. (c) A criterion of correctness is some means of verifying that (more generally, of checking whether) what one is now experiencing is correctly called 'S', that is, of the same sensational type as that initially defined. (d) A criterion of correctness is necessary because in order to use the term 'S' consistently with its definition, as required by (b), one must be able to decide whether one has done so. (e) The private ostensive definition fails to meet the condition (d) (and therefore also (b)) because in the private case one has no means of checking whether or not one is applying the word 'S' consistently with its definition.

All of these elements are clearly present in the best statement of this interpretation: Norman Malcolm's. Imagining a private ostensive definition of 'pain', he writes:

Let us suppose that I did fix my attention on a pain as I pronounced the word 'pain' to myself. I think that thereby I established a connection between the word and the sensation.

But I did not establish a connection if subsequently I applied that word to sensations other than pain or to things other than sensations, e.g. emotions. My private definition was a success only if it led me to use the word correctly in the future. In the present case, 'correctly' would mean '*consistently* with my own definition'. . . . Now how is it to be decided whether I have used the word consistently? What will be the difference between my having used it consistently and its *seeming* to me that I have? Or has this distinction vanished? "Whatever is going to seem right to me is right. And that only means that here we can't talk about 'right'". (Malcolm 1954: 68)

That passage exhibits points (a)–(d). As for the final point (e), Malcolm's view is that one cannot verify that one is using 'S' correctly on the sole basis of one's *impression* that one is doing so. Instead one must have some independent check of that impression itself. And I cannot check my impression against another impression because that would not be an *independent* check. 'As if someone were to buy several copies of the morning paper to assure himself that what it said was true' (PI 265, quoted in Malcolm ibid.). But in the case of the private sensation there *is* no further check, for there are no external signs of S (e.g. typical bodily causes or behavioural effects) by whose occurrence or otherwise one can confirm or disconfirm one's present impression that it is now occurring.

But first, how plausible is point (d)? Why should we not say: it is one thing to use an expression consistently with one's definition but quite another to *know* that one is doing so. Why could the former not happen without the latter? The following example of how it *could* happen is due to Strawson:

[A man] might simply be struck by the recurrence of a certain sensation and get into the habit of making a certain mark in a different place every time it occurred. The making of the marks would help to impress the occurrence on his memory. One can easily imagine this procedure being elaborated into a system of dating. (Strawson 1954: 44)

Or again, a child could be trained – or, we may as well imagine, might magically acquire a habitual tendency – to utter the sound

'S' whenever it feels hot; we could think of this behaviour as a primitive sort of report – just as the behaviour of a thermometer could be thought of as a primitive sort of report on *its* temperature. Nothing in this story requires that the child have any means of checking that it is reporting the same sensational type as the one that we initially connected with 'S'; but still, why should we not call this 'reporting'?

Malcolm's response to Strawson's example is to say that the mere uttering of a sound in the presence of, say, a cow, does not even make that sound into a *word*, let alone a word for *cows*.

> The sound might refer to anything or nothing. What is necessary is that it should play a part in various activities, in calling, fetching, counting cows, distinguishing cows from other things and pictures of cows from pictures of other things. If the sound has no fixed place in activities ('language-games') of this sort, then it isn't a word for *cow*. (Malcolm 1954: 96)

But why must a word or sound play a role in *all* of the activities that Malcolm mentions – or, for that matter, in *any* of them? Why does not Strawson's very light sketch of its use suffice to indicate how 'S' could belong to a language-game of 'reporting one's sensations'? Consider again the very simple builders' language-game at PI 2. There is nothing wrong with saying that 'beam' is a name in that language for beams (cf. PI 37). So the habitual uttering (by A) of 'Slab!' in the presence of a desire for a slab, and the habitual fetching (by B) in the presence of A's utterance, can make 'slab' a name for slabs: why then cannot the mere utterance of 'S' in the presence of S do the same? One could insist if one wished that this pattern of usage is too simple to count as an instance of *our* fully fledged language-game of 'reporting'; but to insist that therefore it cannot count as a report at all is to draw a sharp line around the concept of reporting that an objector to Wittgenstein will refuse to acknowledge.[21]

Nor is it clear that we should accept the verificationist's point (e). It is one thing to say that no *publicly available* occurrence may function as an independent check upon whether one has had S again; it is another thing to say that nothing at all can perform this role. Why should one not be able to check one's impression, that this is S again, against *another* private occurrence? For instance, it may be that whenever I have had sensation S in the past I have also and simultaneously had sensation T. So the presence of T on a later occasion may confirm my impression, on that occasion, that what I am now having is S; and the absence of T on another such occasion may disconfirm my impression, on that other occasion, that what I am now having is S.

The defender of Malcolm will immediately reply that exactly the same problem arises for T itself: how am I to confirm my impression, on any occasion, that I am now having T? (Cf. PI 265: 'checking the same newspaper twice'.) I cannot now appeal to a third type of private occurrence, because that will lead to an infinite regress, and I cannot appeal to S itself, because that would be circular. So I will have to appeal to some publicly available correlate of T, and so the manoeuvre only delays Malcolm's victory.

But the difficulty with this reply is that it presupposes that in order for T to be an independent check on S I must have an independent check on T itself. If that assumption were true the unavailability of a private language would be the least of my problems: for it applies equally to the *public* world. I seem to recall that the word 'desk' applies to this object in front of me, but how can I check? Well, I know that desks have a flat top and four legs. But how can I check whether I am correct to apply 'flat' to the object in front of me? 'Well, desks are usually flat, and what is in front of me is a desk, so . . .' That would be circular. So I must appeal to some third thing: and so again we have an infinite regress. Ayer, to whom this objection is due, summed it up as follows:

[U]nless there is something that one is allowed to recognize, no test can ever be completed: there will be no justification for the use of any sign at all. (Ayer 1954: 256)[22]

And this applies to the private as well as to the public sector of our language.

(ii) *The Meaning-Check*. The second interpretation gives the following answers to our five questions. (a) To 'remember the connection right' is to remember what sensation-type occurred in the *definition* of 'S'. (b) It is necessary to remember the connection right because in order to mean S by 'S' one must know what 'S' means; and one does not know what 'S' means unless one remembers its definition. (c) A criterion of correctness is a means of checking one's memory of the definition of 'S'. (d) A criterion of correctness is necessary because without it one does not remember its definition; and so by (b) one does not know what 'S' means. (e) In the private case one cannot check one's memory of the definition because one has nothing with which to compare it.

The principal difference between the meaning-check interpretation and the verificationist one, from which all the other differences flow, is over question (a). The difference is that the meaning-checker's answer is necessary but not sufficient for the verificationist's: in order to use 'S' consistently with the definition on an occasion, you must be able to remember the *definition*; but one can remember the definition correctly without using 'S' correctly, for one might choose to write something misleading or not to write anything at all (Kenny 1975: 192; Canfield 2001: 384).

In consequence the meaning-checker's answer to question (b) is different from the verificationist's. But it is at least as implausible. It relies on the commonplace but for all that mistaken equation of 'understanding "S"' with '*knowing* the meaning of "S"'. We have already seen (4.1.1) that we can place pressure upon that connection in the interpersonal case: in order to understand another I do not need to *know* but only to have a *true belief* about what he means. But the same point applies to the *intra*personal case: as long as I so much as *guess right* how I defined 'S', I understand it well enough.

Alternatively, my true belief as to what I meant might be the upshot of a causal process whose reliability qualifies that belief as a form of knowledge, at least on a sufficiently externalist conception of our knowledge of the past. That would not be a counterexample to (b); but it would be a counterexample to (d). Thus Kenny, to whom the 'meaning-check' interpretation is due, writes:

Suppose next that the private-language speaker says 'By "S" I mean the sensation I named "S" in the past.' Since he no longer has the past sensation he must rely on memory: he must call up a memory-sample of S and compare it with his current sensation to see if the two are alike. But of course he must call up the *right* memory. Now is it possible that the wrong memory might come at his call? If not, then 'S' means whatever memory occurs to him in connexion with 'S', and . . . whatever seems right to him is right. If so, then he does not really know what he means. (Kenny 1975: 192)

Of course it *is* possible that one should misremember which sensation one named 'S' in the past. But why should the *possibility* of being wrong rule out the *actuality* of knowledge? – 'as if every doubt merely *revealed* an existing gap in the foundations' (PI 87). After all, if one thinks of knowledge as something that a reliable but uncheckable process can produce, then of course one can still remember the definition right, and hence know what it was, whether or not one can check one's memory. And if the meaning-checker should now insist upon so meaning the word 'knowledge' that 'knowledge requires an independent check' is analytic, we are back to the original objection to his point (b).

(3) *Sortalism.* Both verificationism and the meaning-check interpretation take it for granted that the argument is basically epistemological: that what cripples the private diarist's attempt to *mean* something is his not being able to *know* something – for instance, whether 'S' is correctly applied in the present instance. The third interpretation rejects this assumption. Instead the argument is taken to reveal a more basic flaw in the private diarist's procedure. It is not that there is something that he *can't* know, but that there is nothing that he *can*. More precisely: his attempt at a private ostensive definition has failed to specify *any* correct use for the sign 'S', whether or not he could later come to know about it. Even if God had looked into the private linguist's mind he could not have seen there what the sign 'S' was supposed to mean (cf. PI p. 185/217). The reason for this is that the private ostensive definition has not established *which*, of the many types of thing that the initial occurrence of S falls under, is the type or sortal that 'S' is meant to be denoting.

In terms of our five questions, this *sortalist* interpretation may be characterized as follows. (a) To 'remember the connection right' is subsequently to use 'S' in accordance with the pattern of correct use that the initial definition settles. (b) An otherwise satisfactory definition that does not bring this about has not established the meaning of the sign. (c) A criterion of correctness is not a means for the diarist to tell what the correct use is; it is what *makes* this rather than that pattern of use correct. (d) A successful definition must supply such a criterion because otherwise there is no right or wrong use of the sign 'S'. (e) But this cannot happen in the private case because the mere concentration of one's attention upon S while saying 'S' does not make any one pattern of subsequent use more correct than any other, for it does not specify what *type* of thing 'S' is supposed to denote.

In the two clearest and most interesting statements of sortalism – due to McGinn (1997: 131–4) and Stroud (2001): for a briefer account see Glock 1996: 312 – (a) and (b) are stated very briefly or are only implicit; but this is of little importance since it is (c)–(e) that are doing all the work. This is Stroud:

> The speaker [at PI 258] is imagined to give himself an 'ostensive definition' that 'serves to establish' the meaning of a certain sign by impressing on himself 'the connexion' between that sign and a sensation he has at the time he utters it or writes it down . . . It is supposed to be a connection that establishes how the sign is to be correctly used in future. But a word can be 'connected' with one and the same thing in many different ways. To say that 'in the present case I have no criterion of correctness' is to observe that nothing has so far been done to determine which future applications of that sign will be correct and which will not. (2001: 154)

On this interpretation of 'criterion of correctness' he continues:

> The point of there being no 'criterion of correctness' cannot be simply that there is no *test* that the speaker can rely on to tell him that his application of the sign is correct. There is so far nothing for any such test to be a test *for*. Nothing has been done to fix what *being* correct is or would be. (Ibid.)

And on the question of what exactly is undetermined about the future application of 'S' he writes: 'The "overall role" of the sign has not been specified: there is so far no "post" at all at which it is "stationed". It is just a mark written or a sound uttered on a certain occasion' (ibid.).

The words 'post' and 'stationed' in that last remark are allusions to their occurrence in PI 257, which itself is an application to the private sector of the discussion of ostension at PI 28–35 (discussed at 1.2). There Wittgenstein had argued that one could not introduce a name for a colour, a numeral, a point of the compass, and so on unless there was something in virtue of which one had introduced it *as* a name for one kind of thing or another. But what makes it true that the private linguist has introduced the name for, say, the sensation-type that encompasses S rather than for some other type that does so? 'For "sensation" is a word of our common language, not of one intelligible to me alone. So the use of this word stands in need of a justification which everybody understands' (PI 261).

Be that as it may, it is not clear what logical or conceptual difficulty this version of the argument raises for the private diarist. In particular it is not clear what grounds there are for accepting its point (e). Let the diarist utter the sound 'S' in the presence of a sensation on one occasion, and let this occasion be so impressed upon his memory that whenever in future he has something of the *same* sensational type, he then writes 'S' in his diary. There is certainly no need for him to be able to say, in defining S, that it is the name 'for a sensation'; all that is needed is that given his similarity space he responds in similar ways to experiences of the same sensational type. And I cannot see any logical *incoherence* in this possibility (though I have no idea how likely it is).

You might object that we'd have no justification for saying that he was employing 'S' as the sign for a *sensation*. Of course if 'we' is supposed to mean other human beings that is obviously true, for the private language was defined to be one whose terms referred to something that had no external manifestation, so nobody else could tell when it was occurring. To us, it would look as though he was simply writing 'S' in his diary on random days. But that surely does not mean that he is not *in fact* using the sign 'S' as a sign for a sensation. If *God* had looked into his mind then *he* would be justified in so describing it.

The objector might have something else in mind. As we shall see (4.2.5), it was Wittgenstein's view that our everyday words for sensation are 'tied up with' our natural (i.e. bodily) expressions of sensations (PI 256). So, the objector will continue, we cannot say that 'S' is a sign for a sensation because all sensation words stand for states that have natural bodily expressions, and this 'S' has none. (That seems to be the point of a remark at Stroud 2001: 154–5.)

But this argument faces two objections. First, it is hardly clear that our *everyday* words for sensations are 'tied up with' – that is, presumably, require for their understanding an appreciation of – their natural expressions. This is something that, for example, the Lockean will contest; and if the Wittgensteinian is going to defend it then he had better not employ the sortalist version of the private language argument (or his defence will be circular). And second, even if our *everyday* words for sensations *are* so 'tied up with' their natural expressions, it need not be true that *all* sensation words are so tied up in any *possible* language, real or imaginary, natural or artificial. So even in that case the argument would have no logical but at best only inductive force.

It therefore appears that on all of these interpretations the 'private language argument' fails. But we should not give up on it. In addition to these three main interpretations of it, there are others whose distance from these three and each other make one suspect that many treasures (i.e. arguments) remain concealed within PI 258 and its environs. It is too soon to despair of finding one that is actually sound.[23]

4.1.3. The beetle in the box

Whether or not the argument at PI 258 establishes any of the things that I said Wittgenstein there had an interest in showing, the famous 'beetle-in-the-box' argument at PI 293 at least seems to be a clearer and more decisive demonstration of one of them.

We have already seen that on what I have called the 'Lockean' conception, words of our everyday language refer primarily to ideas: that is, objects of quasi-sensory introspection that function as 'inner samples'. Thus with the word 'red' I associate (on this view) an 'inner sample' of red; and if I wish to know, for example, whether this apple is red, what settles the matter for me is a comparison of the inner sample with the outer object. And we have seen how this idea presents a challenge to Wittgenstein's claims about the functional diversity of our words. If one can – as Locke thought – extend this account to all general terms of, say, English ('blue', 'man', 'horse', 'sacrifice', etc.), then one could reasonably insist against Wittgenstein that the superficial diversity in their uses conceals a deeper commonality.

If the Lockean view is right then the words of our everyday public language refer to entities that are in principle quite unknowable to anyone else: at least, nobody can have any evidence for what anybody else has got. If my word 'red' refers to my inner sample of red, and if your word 'red' refers to your inner sample of red, who is to say whether your inner sample is of the same chromatic type as mine?

It may seem at first that we can infer this from the agreement between us in our use of the word 'red', at least in central cases. For instance, we agree that this tomato – which we are observing from the same angle, in the same light, and so on – is red, and we agree that that apple is not red but green. However on the Lockean principle, this agreement might equally be explained in at least two other ways.

(i) If you hold a Lockean theory of perception as well as a Lockean theory of meaning, you will say that what each of us immediately perceives of the apple or tomato is not *it* but the sensory *idea* that it produces in each of us (*Essay* II.ix). So it may be that there is a systematic permutation in the objects of your perception relative to the objects of mine: what produces a green idea in you might produce a red idea in me, while what produces a red idea in you produces a green idea in me. Given that we learn the words 'green', 'red', and so on by being shown objects that are typically said to have those colours, it is therefore likely that you will associate with the word 'red' an idea of the same type as the one that I associate with the word 'green', and vice versa. In that case you would expect our uses of the words 'red' and 'green' to match just as they actually do. And can we rule out that case?

(ii) Wittgenstein himself was correct to say at PI 73 that the inner sample cannot determine one's use of a word by itself: one also needs to use it in a certain way; or, in the terms of PI 139, to have settled upon a *method of projection*. So even if you associate with 'red' an idea of the same chromatic type as the one that I associate with 'green', and vice versa, this difference might still not show up in our uses of 'red' and 'green'. For we might also differ, and in a precisely compensating way, over our methods of projection: so that your 'lines of projection' extend from the idea that you associate with 'red' to tomato ketchup, London buses and post-boxes; whereas mine extend from an idea of the same chromatic type – which, however, I associate with 'green' – to grass, lettuce and the caps worn by Australian cricketers. And conversely, they extend from the idea that I associate with 'red' to tomato ketchup, and so on, and from the idea that *you* associate with 'green' to grass, lettuce, and so on. That is just to say that we associate the same 'inner' ideas with different 'outer' objects, and conversely that we associate different 'inner' ideas with the same 'outer' objects, but in such a way that none of this shows up in our use of the associated words. Indeed this hypothesis would predict just the agreement on overt verbal judgements that we actually observe; on what grounds, then, can we rule it out?

So the Lockean view makes the primary referents of each person's words unknowable to anybody else: at least, it is not something that they can rely upon any evidence to settle. In the terminology of 4.1.1 it makes language out to be epistemically privileged. Only its utterer knows what an utterance of 'red' denotes, for only he knows what idea he associates with it. 'It is as if when I uttered the word I cast a sidelong glance at the private sensation, as it were in order to say to myself: I know all right what I mean by it' (PI 274). It is this aspect of the Lockean view that Wittgenstein's argument fastens upon. It attempts to show that the words of a communal language could not refer to entities that are private in this way.

This is the argument.

Suppose everyone had a box with something in it: we call it a "beetle". No one can look into anyone else's box, and everyone says he knows what a beetle is only by looking at *his* beetle. – Here it would be quite possible for everyone to have something different in his box. One might even imagine such a thing constantly changing. – But suppose the word "beetle" had a use in these people's language? – If so it would not be used as the name of a thing. The thing in the box has no place in the language-game at all; not even as a *something*: for the

box might even be empty. – No, one can 'divide through' by
the thing in the box; it cancels out, whatever it is.

That is to say: if we construe the grammar of the expression
of sensation on the model of 'object and designation' the
object drops out of consideration as irrelevant. (PI 293b–c)

The intention of the analogy is fairly clear. The beetle corresponds
to the inner or private idea that we are each supposed to associate with, for example, some sensation word of English, to which
latter the word 'beetle' corresponds. And the point is that the
public use of the expression 'beetle', whatever it is, does not
depend upon what is in anyone's box. For its public use would
proceed undisturbed if each of us had a different object in his
box; indeed it might proceed undisturbed if some of us had
nothing in the box. So in its public use the word 'beetle' in somebody's hand or mouth does not refer to his beetle; and the
analogous conclusion goes for sensation words – and indeed
all other words – of an everyday language like English, that is,
one that has many speakers.

Let us first distinguish this point from what the argument
does *not* show. It does not show – nor, I think, does it attempt to
show – that the words 'red', 'green', and so on could not have a
private meaning *in addition* to their public one. But what it does
try to show is that if we focus solely upon the public usage of
these words, that is, the use upon which we all agree, we can
eliminate all reference to private objects in the explanation of *it*.
That would be enough to defeat the Lockean challenge to PI 1
that I mentioned at 1.1. It would show that we should not see the
public uses of different words as superficially dissimilar tips of
similar icebergs; rather, those 'tips' are each quite disconnected
from whatever lies beneath the surface.

But does it show *this* much? There can be no question, I think,
that the argument illustrates pretty clearly that one may vary
one's inner objects without varying the public use, in some
sense of 'use', of the associated word. But what do we mean
here by 'use'?

Wittgenstein nowhere makes it precise, but I think that in
order properly to assess this argument we must do so. At any
rate we must make precise what counts as 'the same use'. Let
us say, then, that a person's *public use* of a word is the totality

of his dispositions to utter, and to assent to, or dissent from, sentences containing that word, in response to given sensory stimulations. For instance, it belongs to my public use of the word 'red' that I am disposed to assent to the query 'Red?' when confronted with a visibly salient ripe tomato; and it further belongs to my public use of that word that I am disposed to say 'Red!' when queried about its colour shortly thereafter. (In the terminology of 3.2.1 I am speaking here of a person's A-dispositions, not his B-dispositions.) And just as you would expect, we shall say that two people have the *same public use* for a word if and only if the use that one of them has for it is the same as the use that the other one has for it.

This is a highly artificial and certainly not very Wittgensteinian definition of 'public use' and 'same public use'. Moreover, it makes it very unlikely that two people will ever have the same public use for a word. For it makes one's use of a word depend in part upon what would usually be reckoned collateral information as opposed to knowledge of that word's meaning. For instance, in response to the question 'Was Lyndon Johnson the thirty-sixth President of the United States?' A might be disposed to say 'Yes' whereas B is disposed to say 'No'; on the present definition it follows that A and B have different public uses for 'thirty-six'.

But neither of these points is going to matter. For one thing, my artificial version of 'public use' does no disservice to Wittgenstein in the present context. If the beetle in the box cannot be made to establish its intended conclusion by means of *this* conception of sameness of public use, then I do not see how it can be made to work at all. And second, the fact that my definition makes it very unlikely that two people will ever have the same public use for a word makes no real difference either. It means that one of the premises that I attribute to Wittgenstein is going to seem very strong; but it will induce a compensating weakness in the other premise, so the overall soundness of the argument will not be affected.

So on this conception of sameness of public use, the argument *does* show that two people might have the same public use for an expression while associating it with different private objects. For instance, A and B might associate quite different private objects with the word 'toothache'. But *still* they might both have exactly the same public use for the word. For instance, they could and would both go to the dentist complaining of 'toothache', and he could and would treat them appropriately in response, for example, by extracting the rotten tooth. What is in the box cancels out.

But it does not show that just *any* variation of the private object would be immaterial to one's use of the word. Suppose that somebody associated the *same* inner object and the *same* 'method of projection' with the words 'green' and 'red'. In that case the inner object would *not* cancel out: there would have to be a difference between his and our usage of at least one of the words 'red' and 'green'. For *he* would apply 'red' to ripe tomatoes if and only if he applied 'green' to ripe tomatoes; whereas we apply 'red' only to *ripe* tomatoes and 'green' only to *unripe* ones.

What the argument shows, then, is that we can preserve the public use of words while varying the inner object *ad libitum* so long as we make compensating variations elsewhere. In particular the variation must assign different inner objects (or, if you like, different inner-objects-plus-methods-of-projection) to words that were initially assigned to different ones, and it must for the same reasons assign the same inner objects to words that were initially assigned to the same ones. Such a variation is called an *injection* of the inner objects. So we can put it like this: Wittgenstein has shown that an injection of the inner objects associated with our public words is immaterial to their public use.

But this is not yet the intended conclusion of the beetle-in-the-box argument. The intended conclusion is the one stated at PI 293c: that none of these words actually denote any inner object. So does *this* claim follow from the premise that an injection of the inner objects associated with our public words is immaterial to their public use?

It does not follow logically, but it *does* follow on the additional assumption of a premise that Wittgenstein shows every sign of accepting (short of actually stating it). This premise can be put as a slogan: no variation in reference without variation in use. Wittgenstein actually comes fairly close to endorsing it with the remark that 'the word "name" is used to characterize many different kinds of *use* of a word' (PI 38b; my emphasis). But this does not quite count as an endorsement of what I mean, if only because Wittgenstein nowhere gives to 'same use' the precise meaning that I have assigned it for present purposes.[24] In any case it seems quite clearly to be in the spirit of Wittgenstein's general idea that semantic phenomena are not independent of but arise wholly from one's use of words. More precisely, the premise is this: there could not be two people who had the same public use for words that yet had different references. We may term this premise 'semantic behaviourism'.[25]

But PI 293b has shown that there could be two people who had the same public use for a word (like 'beetle') that was associated with different inner objects. It follows from our two premises that that word cannot refer to either associated inner object. Since both word and object were arbitrary, we can generalize the conclusion of this argument: *no* word of a public language refers to *any* associated inner object. It therefore seems that the argument has successfully established the conclusion that it states at PI 293c.

But one might ask whether it has thereby pointed out any special difficulty about reference to *private* objects. After all, we could make the very same point about public objects; Quine has done so.[26] Let us suppose that every object has a *complement*. The complement of an object O is the object O* that is composed of the entirety of the universe (all of space and time) *except* for that object (so O** = O). Now imagine two people A and B: A associates his words with ordinary physical objects – 'tomato' with tomatoes, 'Fido' with Fido, 'dog' with dogs, and so on – whereas B associates those words with their complements – 'tomato' with complements of tomatoes, 'Fido' with Fido*, 'dog' with the complements of dogs, and so on. Clearly, replacing all objects with their complements is an injection of those objects, in the sense of 'injection' defined earlier.

Now on certain simplifying assumptions B will assent to (e.g.) 'Fido is a dog' if and only if Fido* is a complement of a dog, that is, if and only if Fido is a dog, that is, if and only if A will assent to the same sentence given the same evidence. What happens is that the variation in B on what A associates with 'Fido' exactly compensates for the variation in B on what A associates with 'dog'. And I believe that this point can be generalized; so it is possible that A and B should have the same public use for all of their words. That is, one may vary by injection a set of *outer* objects while the public use of the associated words proceeds quite undisturbed.

Applying now the premise of semantic behaviourism (which has no special application to *inner* objects) and generalizing the result as in the private case we may conclude that no word of a public language refers to any associated *outer* object. The outer object cancels out in just the same way as the inner one.

So Wittgenstein's argument, at least on this construal of it, does not after all reveal any *special* problem with the Lockean idea that one's words denote associated private objects. Now it may be that the problem resides in my reading of the argument. In particular and for the purpose of assessing it, I assigned to the notion of 'sameness of public use' a definition that Wittgenstein would quite possibly not have accepted. Could he have had in mind some other notion of 'public use' than the brute behavioural propensities with which I there identified it?

Quite possibly he did; but it is not clear how that would help him. Whatever notion of 'use' he may have had in mind, the argument at PI 293b appears to show quite effectively that variation of associated objects is compatible with sameness of use *in my sense as well* as his. So PI 293b does successfully establish my reading of the first premise, whatever else it establishes.

And whatever notion of use he may have had in mind is surely one that cuts no finer than mine: two people who have the same public use for a word in my sense will have the same public use for it in *any* sense of that Protean word. It follows that if semantic behaviourism is true on his interpretation of 'same public use' then it is true on mine as well. So if the second premise of *his* argument is correct, whatever it may be, then so is the second premise of my reading of it.

So if Wittgenstein's beetle-in-the-box argument establishes the semantical irrelevance of inner objects then it establishes the semantical irrelevance of outer ones too. Hence it establishes no *special* difficulty for a Lockean interpretation of our language on which words denote associated private or inner objects. What is wrong with the beetle-in-the-box argument is not that it fails to establish its conclusion. It is that one could travel much further in its direction; from the perspective that one then attains, Wittgenstein's limitation of his argument to the private sector looks arbitrary.[27]

4.2. The inner and the outer

The two passages that this chapter has so far focused upon are embedded within a much larger discussion of a variety of misconceptions that affect philosophical thinking about sensations and indeed the whole picture of our mental life. Those misconceptions coalesce into what might with some historical license be called the Cartesian picture, although in using this label one should bear in mind that it has probably shaped the thoughts of many people who were not Descartes to a greater extent than it ever informed the work of that great philosopher, and that among these people were philosophers with whom he was not otherwise in intellectual sympathy.

Having outlined this picture we shall discuss various points at which Wittgenstein attacked it: (a) the idea that their bearer has a special epistemic authority over his sensational states; (b) the idea that we are inevitably in a state of *ignorance* as to somebody else's sensational states; (c) the idea that their bearer is a self or soul that is distinct from one's body; (d) the idea that we come to understand third-personal sensational attributions by a transference of our understanding in the first-personal case. I conclude with a discussion of Wittgenstein's alternative to (d).

4.2.1. The Cartesian picture

The basic Cartesian picture is that from the point of view of any human individual, for instance me, the world is open to being metaphysically factored into two logically independent components. On the one hand there is the physical or 'external' world (though it is slightly misleading to call it 'external' as it includes the interior of my body as well as my brain). At least in principle everyone has equally good observational access to this world. It is true that in practice there are some parts of it that I am in a better position to observe than anyone else. For instance, I can feel the goings-on in my muscles better than anybody else can see them, so I am in a better position to observe a cramp in them than anyone else. But at least in principle another observer could observe that cramp by looking at my muscles; in fact in principle somebody else's nerves might be connected to my muscle, in which case that other person would be as well-placed as me to *feel* the cramp.

On the other hand there is the mental or internal world. This is the world of mental states, processes and events: sensations, feelings, moods – but also thoughts, beliefs and preferences. *In principle* I have better access to my own mental states than anybody else. In particular my sensations are objects of direct internal observation, by which I have infallible access to them. I cannot be mistaken about my sensations. My knowledge of them therefore has a security to which my knowledge of the merely external world can never attain.

But nobody else can observe them directly. This is not because they are hidden within my skull: even if my head had been made of glass, so that other people could see everything that was going on in my brain, they would still not be observing my sensations. So other people have to make an inference about my sensations upon the basis of what they do observe: in practice this is my behaviour.

And what is this 'I' that observes these sensational states? It is not my body or any mere state of my body. It is a spiritual entity called the 'self' that directly observes just the sensations that it 'owns'. There are many such selves, each one corresponding to a person, and each one has 'its' sensations that *it* observes directly and which no other self observes directly. But the self can understand what it is for another self to have a sensation by concentrating on its own. 'Jones's having toothache', Smith might say to himself, 'is just another occurrence of *this* [here concentrating on his own toothache], only an occurrence that Jones owns, not me.'

This picture is not some medley of ideas that Descartes happened to throw together. There are indisputable facts that make it very natural for many people (at least for many Westerners) to think in terms of it without ever making it explicit. Wittgenstein's treatment of the picture is an attempt to extract it by these roots.

4.2.2 *The epistemic asymmetry*
We have seen that one important component of the Cartesian picture is the idea that I know, for example, whether I am feeling a headache right now; everybody else has to infer it. In connection with this epistemic asymmetry Wittgenstein writes:

> In what sense are my sensations *private*? – Well, only I can know whether I am really in pain; another person can only

surmise it. – In one way this is wrong, and in another nonsense. If we are using the word "to know" as it is normally used (and how else are we to use it?), then other people very often know when I am in pain. – Yes, but all the same not with the certainty with which I know it myself! – It can't be said of me at all (except perhaps as a joke) that I *know* I am in pain. What is it supposed to mean – except perhaps that I *am* in pain?

Other people cannot be said to learn of my sensations *only* from my behaviour, – for *I* cannot be said to learn of them. I *have* them.

The truth is: it makes sense to say about other people that they doubt whether I am in pain; but not to say it about myself. (PI 246)

Let us start with my knowledge of my own sensations. Wittgenstein asks what it might mean to say that I know that I am in pain – other than that I *am* in pain. But why should we think that these two statements mean the same? After all, they have different *uses*. I might say 'I am in pain' to the dentist when he is extracting my tooth as a way to indicate that he should administer more anaesthetic. But I'd only say 'I *know* that I am in pain!' if the dentist started to question my first statement: 'Are you sure that you feel pain?', and so on.

Wittgenstein thinks that 'I know I am in pain' does not mean anything *else* because knowledge-statements are not true in cases where it makes no sense to doubt. He writes elsewhere that

"I know . . ." may mean "I do not doubt . . ." but does not mean that the words "I doubt . . ." are *senseless*, that doubt is logically excluded. (PI p. 188/p. 221)

And as he says at PI 246c it seems that this is one of those cases in which the expression of doubt is senseless or logically excluded. At least it is so in this sense: somebody who sincerely said 'I doubt whether I am in pain' would thereby reveal nothing except his misunderstanding of one of those words: he might think, for instance, that 'pain' names a certain type of bodily damage.

But in that sense of logical exclusion, utterances of 'It is raining' on a plainly sunny day are logically excluded too: somebody who sincerely said that should be taken to have misunderstood *his* words. But then the fact that a statement is logically excluded cannot rule out the sensefulness and indeed truth of its negation. 'It is not raining' would on that occasion say something so obvious as to make its utterance pointless; but for all that it would say something *true*. Why then should 'I know that I am in pain' not say something true as well?

Another reason for thinking that 'I know that I am in pain' cannot mean anything other than 'I am in pain' is that 'I am in pain' is not something that one can *either* know *or* believe, because it is not a description of anything at all but simply a means of attracting attention disguised as an assertion. This may be part of what Wittgenstein had in mind when he wrote that the verbal expression of pain replaces crying (PI 244; cf. PI 290b). Obviously it does not make sense to affix 'I believe . . .' or 'I know . . .' before a *cry*; perhaps then we ought to say the same about the statement got by affixing either before 'I am in pain'.

But we have good reason to think that this is something that one can believe. The point of attributing beliefs to people is to explain their behaviour; but there are plenty of things that I can do that make it pointful to attribute that belief to me. Suppose that walking into a room I learn that at least one other person in it is in pain; and I infer (i.e. form the belief) that at least two people in the room are in pain. Couldn't it be a good explanation of this that I already believe that *I* am in pain? In that case, 'I am in pain' expresses what someone might be said to believe; why then shouldn't it express what someone might be said to *know*?

Let us turn now to *other* people's knowledge of my pain. Wittgenstein said that if we are using the word 'to know' as it is ordinarily used ('and how else are we to use it?'), then other people very often know when I am in pain. As an empirical report on ordinary usage I dare say that this is true. It is certainly much easier to think of likely scenarios in which an ordinary speaker of English would say '*Johnny* knows that I am in pain' than it is to think of ones in which he or she would say '*I* know that I am in pain.'

But why think that what people say frequently must be taken literally, or that, if so taken, it must be true? Imagine someone arguing like this: 'If we are using the words "to rise" and "to set" as they are normally used (and how else are we to use them?), then the sun rises and sets every day.' The natural response to this would be that there is a way of using the words 'to rise' and 'to set' that does not slavishly adhere to the sprawling mass of their ordinary usages but attempts to extract a concept from some subset of their 'literal' uses (as suggested at 2.3).

In fact doing so is *itself* no departure from ordinary usage. For most ordinary but educated speakers will acknowledge such a literal core: confronted with the astronomical evidence they will concede that of course the sun doesn't *really* rise and set, and that this is just a manner of speaking. But then why should we not say the same about knowledge of other minds? After all, confronted with the 'philosophical evidence', most ordinary speakers will concede: 'Of course one doesn't ever *really* know what another person is feeling when his tooth is rotten: I just assume that he is feeling the same as I do.' Wittgenstein's point therefore relies on there being some weakness in that philosophical evidence, to which we now turn.

The traditional problem of our knowledge of other minds arises directly from the Cartesian picture itself. According to that picture, Jones can never observe my pain; he can only ever infer that I am in pain from premises about my behaviour whose truth he *does* observe: 'A. A. is exhibiting pain-behaviour, therefore he is in pain.' But then the question arises: with what right does Jones make *that* inference? After all he has never observed it to have been confirmed by any of its instances: that is, he has never been in a position to observe, on the one hand my pain-behaviour, and on the other hand my pain. It is only observations of that sort that would justify his concluding that very often A. A.'s pain accompanied his pain-behaviour, thereby warranting the problematic inference. *I* am the only person who is in a position to make observations of that sort. But that is not going to be of any help to Jones: for even if I made those observations, my report of the results – 'A. A. is in pain on $n\%$ of the occasions on which he exhibits pain-behaviour' – will not confirm the problematic inference for Jones without the help of an equally problematic inference from 'A. A. reports that he was in pain on an occasion' to 'A. A. *was* in pain on that occasion.' For how can Jones rule out the hypothesis that I call 'pain' what he calls 'pleasure' (see 4.1.3)?

Of course what Jones *can* observe on the Cartesian picture is his *own* case: and he can summarize the results in the form 'Jones is in pain on *m*% of the occasions on which he exhibits pain-behaviour.' But however great *m* is, this might seem to be very weak inductive grounds on which to extend the inference from *others'* pain-behaviour to their pain. It would be as rash as it would be for one of the characters in PI 293 to infer, from the observation of a black stag beetle in his own box, that everyone else's box contained a black stag beetle.

There is therefore a reasonable case for thinking that Jones does *not* really know whether I am in pain. This case certainly recommends divergence from the 'ordinary use' of the word 'know', but not an arbitrary divergence. It is rather that it combines principles about knowledge that ordinary speakers would in any case acknowledge – for instance, that if an inference yields knowledge then it must have a sound evidential base – with premises taken from the Cartesian picture – for instance, that Jones cannot observe my pain – and seems to establish that on a sense of 'know' that respects these principles, there is indeed no knowledge of other minds.

The appeal to the ordinary use of 'know' at PI 246 therefore does nothing to legitimize others' knowledge of my sensations. However Wittgenstein does raise a further difficulty with the argument that such knowledge is impossible. This objection strikes at the heart of Cartesian picture. It is that that picture, and the scepticism about other minds that follows from it, rest upon a misunderstanding of the ordinary concept – not of knowledge but – of *pain*. I shall discuss this point at 4.2.4; but a proper explanation of it requires a brief discussion of Wittgenstein's views on the self.

4.2.3. *The self*
On the Cartesian picture your understanding of 'I am in pain' involved a correlation on the one hand between 'pain' and an inner object, and on the other hand between 'I' and an inner subject – your *self*, the owner of these states. You are in pain whenever that object stands in the right relation to that subject.

Apart from Descartes himself the most important writer on this subject is Hume, who notoriously pointed out that when he 'enters into his own experience' he never encounters any such owner but only the sensations themselves (*Treatise* I.iv.6). Wittgenstein seems to have endorsed this reasoning in the *Tractatus*:

> If I wrote a book called *The World as I found it*, I should have to include a report on my body, and should have to say which parts were subordinate to my will, and which were not, etc., this being a method of isolating the subject, or rather of showing that in an important sense there is no subject; for it alone could not be mentioned in that book. (TLP 5.631)

But the reader should note that in the *Tractatus* he also believed in a 'metaphysical' self (TLP 5.641) that was not found in experience: rather, it was the thing whose mental acts were what infused its symbolic thought-processes with meaning: the thing that somehow correlates names with their referents by means of the method of projection (TLP 3.11). Language is *my* language – the language that *I* infuse with meaning; so language itself is a sort of immanent reflection of a thinking subject. That was why he felt able to write:

> The limits of my language mean the limits of my world . . . The world is my world: this is manifest in the fact that the limits of *language* (of that language which alone I understand) mean the limits of *my* world. (TLP 5.6, 5.62)[28]

By the time of the *Investigations* Wittgenstein had partially revised his earlier attitude. On the one hand, he no longer agreed that a metaphysical self was a necessary condition of meaning: as we saw at section 3 the 'act of meaning' or 'act of projection' was a fiction: what turns a dead sign into a meaningful symbol is its *use* and not 'a hocus-pocus which can be performed only by the soul' (PI 454). On the other hand, he still sympathized with the Humean argument expressed in the passage quoted from TLP 5.631, or at any rate with its conclusion. That is, he thought that when I say 'I am in pain' there is no thing to which I attribute that property:

> "When I say 'I am in pain' [says the interlocutor], I do not point to a person who is in pain, since in a certain sense I have

no idea *who* is." And this can be given a justification. For the
main point is: I did not say that such-and-such a person was
in pain, but "I am . . . . ." Now in saying this I don't name any
person. Just as I don't name anyone when I *groan* with pain.
Though someone else sees who is in pain from the groaning.
(PI 404)

"I" is not the name of a person (PI 410)

Why is 'I' not the name of a person? One reason might be the
Humean thought to which I just alluded: that there is no self or
soul if by that we mean an immaterial subject of sensations. But
this argument is not quite sufficient: for it leaves it open that 'I'
is the name of my body and that *that* is a person. On the other
hand, that proposal can't be right either, because if 'I' were the
name of my body then 'I am feeling such-and-such' could not be
uttered truly by someone who felt such-and-such outside of his
body, for instance in another's body (PI 302a, PI 409) or at the
end of a stick (PI 626).[29]
What then *is* the function of 'I' in the context 'I am in pain'?
It exploits the fact that the mouth that speaks and the hand that
writes are causally connected with unique closeness to a discrete
organic body. This allows for the existence of conventions by
which the behaviour of the mouth and hand can be especially
closely associated with, for example, ailments of that body . So
when a mouth says 'I am in pain' we know which body needs
treatment – the body that is attached to that mouth. Thus the
function of the word 'I' in 'I am in pain' is to attract people's
attention to a particular body.
Now we have already seen that this connection need not be
invariable. One might certainly feel pain in some distant part of
the world from one's mouth; indeed that was the reason for
doubting that 'I' *names* the body that feels pain. But were this
contingent fact *never* to obtain we should have no occasion to
speak of 'my' pains or to say 'I am in pain'. Were it the case that,
somewhat like the three witches in the story, we all took turns to
speak through a single mouth in central London, to which we
were each connected by radio receivers and radio transmitters,
this mouth would never say, for example, 'I am in pain' or speak
of 'my' pains – at any rate there would be no point in its doing

so. Instead it would say things like 'There is pain at 36 Ramsey Street, Glasgow' – and then people would attend to the bodies in that place. Here we are imagining certain very general facts of nature to be different; doing so makes intelligible the formation of very different concepts from ours (PI II, xii: p. 195).

But given that the facts of nature are as they are we can see that the first-person present tense sentence 'I am in pain' serves the same function as a cry – to draw people's attention to a certain body. And that is Wittgenstein's account of it: 'I am in pain' does not *describe* a cry but *replaces* one (PI 244).

Bearing all of this in mind, let us now turn to the concept of pain, and in particular to our expression of it by means of third-personal sensation ascriptions.

4.2.4. Third-personal sensation ascriptions:
The negative account

What underlies the Cartesian idea about epistemic asymmetry is an idea about what I am doing when I attribute sensations to somebody else. This idea can be expressed as a thesis about how we come to grasp such third-personal ascriptions. It is that each of us initially grasps what it is to *be* in pain, say: that is, we initially master the first-personal avowal of pain. And then we come to grasp its third-personal counterpart via the reflection that for *Johnny* to be in pain is for *him* to have just what *I* have when *I* am in pain. On this very natural account there is nothing especially mysterious about the move from an understanding of the first-personal to an understanding of the third-personal sensation language. It is just a special case of the more general competence that we have – and which we exhibit in other cases – of moving from an understanding of what is mine to an understanding of what is another's.

Thus Billy might first learn the difference between things that are and things that are not '*his* toys': he is in a position to exercise certain rights over his toys that he is not in a position to exercise over other toys. And then he comes to understand that certain toys are and certain toys are not '*Johnny's* toys' by a process of abstraction of himself from the concept of '*his* toys': namely, what he learns is that Johnny's toys are just those toys to which *Johnny* stands in the very same proprietary relations that he (Billy) stands to *his* toys.

According to the Cartesian the step from 'my pain' to 'Johnny's pain' proceeds in essentially the same way. To understand sensation terms is in the first instance to understand that they denote inner objects to which you stand in a special relation – these are *my* pains, *my* afterimages, and so on; and one extends one's under-standing to the third-personal case when one learns that 'Johnny's pain' denotes objects that are inner to Johnny, that is, objects to which *Johnny* stands in the same relation as you do to *your* pains.

But recall our discussion in the preceding section. We saw there that the function of 'I' in the case of first-personal avowals was not to name any thing but rather to draw people's attention to the mouth (and associated body) that says it. Now if that is the function of 'I' in contexts like 'I am in pain' then it is evident that mastery of the latter does not demand acquaintance with – or any other knowledge of – some relation between a type of inner object (the pain) and an inner subject (the 'self' that 'has it'), from which latter one may then abstract so as to move from a grasp of 'I am in pain' to a grasp of 'Johnny is in pain'. In order that 'I am in pain' function in the manner just sketched, it is necessary only that mastery of it involve (roughly) a disposition to utter it when and only when certain bodily events occur in the body that is attached to your mouth. But this means that mastery of 'I am in pain' does not give you the resources to move by abstraction to mastery of 'Johnny is in pain'. For you have no idea at all of what you are supposed to be abstracting *from*.

Thus Wittgenstein writes:

> If one has to imagine someone else's pain on the model of one's own, this is none too easy a thing to do: for I have to imagine pain which I *do not feel* on the model of the pain which I *do feel*. That is, what I have to do is not simply to make a transition in imagination from one place of pain to another. As, from pain in the hand to pain in the arm. For I am not to imagine that I feel pain in some region of his body. (Which would also be possible.) (PI 302)

And this is the point of the famous comparison with '5 o'clock on the sun':

> "But if I suppose that someone has a pain [says the interlocutor], then I am simply supposing that he has just the same as I have

so often had." – That gets us no further. It is as if I were to say: "You surely know what 'It is 5 o'clock here' means; so you also know what 'It's 5 o'clock on the sun' means. It means simply that it is just the same there as it is here when it is 5 o'clock." – The explanation by means of *identity* does not work here. For I know well enough that one can call 5 o'clock here and 5 o'clock there "the same time", but what I do not know is in what cases one is to speak of its being the same time here and there. (PI 350)

According to the Cartesian picture I observe both pain and myself when I am in pain; what I am to do is then to suppose that for Johnny to be in pain is for another subject to have that same relation to that same object as I do when I am in pain. Against this we can see in the preceding passages the consequences of Wittgenstein's rejection of the subject of pain: since the 'I' in 'I am in pain' doesn't refer to any subject there is no reason to think that we can understand 'Johnny is in pain' by regarding it as simply a variation upon the subject but not upon the object of 'I am in pain'. That is the point of the comparison with '5 o'clock on the sun': since our understanding of temporal expressions of the form 'It is 5 o'clock at x' extends only to cases where x denotes a place on the surface of the Earth, there is no reason to think that we can understand 'It is 5 o'clock on the sun' by regarding it as simply a variation upon the location but not upon the time of, for example, 'It is 5 o'clock at Greenwich.'

4.2.5. *Third-personal sensation ascriptions:*
The positive account

How then *do* we understand third-personal ascriptions of sensation? Wittgenstein writes that 'an 'inner process' stands in need of outward criteria' (PI 580) and it is by the criteria of pain – its natural and involuntary behavioural manifestations – that we tell whether to ascribe it.

It is worth briefly saying something at this point about Wittgenstein's notion of a *criterion*. Let us distinguish between two sorts of evidence for a given type of state of affairs. One sort of evidence depends, for its status *as* evidence, upon an observed correlation between itself and what it is evidence *for*;

that is to say, it would cease to count as evidence were we to find out that a relatively high proportion of cases in which the evidence was present were ones in which the state of affairs was *absent*.

An example of this sort of evidence is the barometer, whose prediction of rain is only defeasibly evidence for rain. If we observed on enough occasions that the rain did not succeed the barometer's prediction of it we should eventually cease to rely upon the barometer as a means for predicting rain. The fact that this could happen illustrates the sense in which the barometer's behaviour is only defeasibly evidence for future rain.

But another sort of evidence does *not* depend upon its status as evidence for something upon such an observed correlation between it and the thing it is evidence for; its status as evidence is *a priori* (or, as Wittgenstein says at PI 354, founded upon a definition). Let us consider the status of pain-behaviour as evidence for pain. What sort of evidence could make us doubt that pain-behaviour (among humans) really was evidence for their being in pain? The answer is: none. Instead we should doubt the status as such of the 'evidence' that indicated (e.g.) that there was *no* pain in the *presence* of pain-behaviour, or that there *was* pain in its *absence*.

Evidence of the first sort is what Wittgenstein means by a 'symptom'. Evidence of the second sort is what he means by a 'criterion'. (He contrasts the two at PI 354.) Note well that a criterion for a state of affairs may itself be *defeasible* evidence for that state of affairs, that is, not sufficient for it;[30] what is indefeasible is its status *as* evidence.

And it is clear that pain-behaviour is a criterion of pain. For – given that our concept of pain is as it is – nothing could count as evidence against *that* evidential link. Such 'evidence' might look like this: when you hit somebody with a hammer he does not cry out or make any antagonistic response; and he does nothing to avoid hammer blows in the future. On the other hand when you gave him strawberries for the first time he winces and then retaliates (by hitting you), and he *does* exhibit strawberry-avoiding behaviour thereafter. Nobody who observed this case would conclude that his pain-behaviour was not after all evidence of his pain. Rather, he would conclude that what hurts *us* does not hurt *him* (and vice versa).

Here then is Wittgenstein's account of third-personal sensation ascriptions. A speaker learns them by learning their criteria. What you learn is the kind of behaviour that counts as pain-behaviour (and in the case of other sensational states you learn *their* criteria, which might, for example, be their causes or their effects). And your mastery of the term 'pain' involves being able to distinguish pain-behaviour from other sorts of behaviour, and treating the former as defeasible grounds for asserting that the other person is in pain. To master the ascription of 'pain' on these grounds is to master our concept of pain, at least in third-personal contexts.

Obviously there is a good deal more to be said about that account, but we are now in a position to say something more about the problem of our knowledge of other minds. In the passage that distinguishes criteria from symptoms Wittgenstein makes an analogous point in connection with visual impressions. He writes:

> We say, for example: "Experience teaches that there is rain when the barometer falls, but it also teaches that there is rain when we have certain sensations of wet and cold, or such-and-such visual impressions." In defence of this one says that these sense-impressions may deceive us. But here one fails to reflect that the fact that the false appearance is precisely one of rain is founded on a definition. (PI 354)

> The point here is not that our sense-impressions may lie, but that we understand their language. (And this language like any other is founded on convention.) (PI 355)

The application to other minds ought to be clear. The problem was supposed to be that Jones cannot have any reason for thinking that I am in pain because he cannot observe my pain. The answer is that it is part of the *concept* of pain that Jones can have such reasons, namely, my pain-behaviour. And somebody who sincerely doubts whether my pain-behaviour is at least *grounds* for ascribing pain to me has also failed to grasp the concept. That is because pain-behaviour is *criterial* for pain.

It is clear that this account of third-personal sensation ascriptions completely upsets the Cartesian picture that gave rise to the problem in the first place. But it is also clear that it threatens to cut certain very natural lines of thought that would otherwise continue to nourish the Cartesian conception. Because Wittgenstein's treatment of these lines of thought connects these topics with other central themes in both the *Tractatus* and *Philosophical Investigations*, I shall conclude by considering two.

4.2.6. *'Pain is pain'*

The most obvious objection to Wittgenstein's account is that it has omitted something utterly crucial to our third-personal ascriptions of 'pain'. We have seen that one does not 'imagine someone else's pain on the model of one's own' (PI 302). But Wittgenstein's account seems to go too far in the opposite direction. He seems to imply that one imagines someone else's pain on the model of something *completely different from* one's own. For we have two things: the pain that I feel when I say that *I* am in pain, and the pain-behaviour that Jones shows when I say that *he* is in pain. These two things are entirely different; so it looks as if my grounds for making statements of the form *x is in pain* are irremediably disjunctive.

So on Wittgenstein's account of it, it is starting to look as though the word 'pain' is simply ambiguous between its first- and third-personal uses. So nothing would be lost from my language if I instituted *different* words for each. And Wittgenstein does seem willing to draw this startling conclusion.

> If I were to reserve the word "pain" solely for what I had hitherto called "my pain", and others "L. W.'s pain", I should do other people no injustice, so long as a notation were provided in which the loss of the word "pain" in other connexions were somehow supplied. Other people would still be pitied, treated by doctors and so on. It would, of course, be *no* objection to this mode of expression to say: "But look here, other people have just the same as you!" (PI 403)

Of course it is *correct* to say that they have 'just the same as me' (because it is correct, at least in English, to say 'they have pain' and correct to say 'I have pain') but that does not mean that something in the objects themselves – the intrinsic nature of their pains and our pains – forces upon us a notation that employs the same expression for both. But does this not make 'pain' comparable to 'bank'? Of course the ambiguity of 'pain' would not quite be the same as that of 'bank', because it is primarily in one kind of context (the first-personal one) that 'pain' has one meaning and it is primarily in another kind of context (the third-personal one) that 'pain' has another meaning – the one we learn by coming to appreciate its criteria. On the other hand just one occurrence of 'bank' can have different meanings ('I visited the bank'). Perhaps a better comparison would be between the word 'pain' and the word 'March' (the name of the month and the order): the contexts in which it takes one meaning have little to do with those in which it takes another; still it is correctly described as a mere accident of our language that the word 'March' can in these contexts denote quite different kinds of thing. Given Wittgenstein's semantics for 'pain', must we not then describe it – most implausibly – as a mere accident of (probably all) human languages that any expression that has the first-person use of the English word also has its *third*-person use?

One central thesis of the *Tractatus* entailed a positive answer to this question. According to that book the grammatical behaviour of a word was dictated by the nature of the simple object that it denoted, and to know the object is to know *all* of its possible occurrences in states of affairs (2.0123). Now the possibility of the notation of PI 403 would indicate to the author of the *Tractatus* that somebody could know what 'pain' in that language denoted, that is, what pain was, without knowing that other people, too, might be in pain. But that means that the word 'pain' as it occurs in English has 'different modes of signification, and so belongs to different symbols' (TLP 3.323); and in the case of such accidental ambiguities 'we must make use of a sign-language that excludes them by not using the same sign for different symbols' (TLP 3.325). That is, if we can use a language like that of PI 403 then – from a logical point of view – we *must*.

In *Philosophical Investigations* Wittgenstein addresses this question in a sequence that includes the following statement of it:

But how can I decide what is an essential, and what an inessential, accidental, feature of the notation? Is there some reality lying behind the notation, which shapes its grammar? (PI 562)

A little later he raises the question in a way that has direct application to pain. And he returns a preliminary answer:

> Why the same word? In the calculus we make no use of this identity! . . . – But what does it mean here to speak of "making use of the identity"? For isn't it a use, if we do in fact use the same word? (PI 565)

But that is quite unsatisfactory. You might as well say that we 'make use of the identity' of the word for the depositing and lending institution on the one hand and for the sloped ground by a river on the other – for don't we use the same word ('bank') for each of *them*? There is then another suggestion:

> And now it looks as if the use of the same word or the same piece [i.e. in a game] had a *purpose* – if the identity is not accidental, inessential. And as if the purpose were that one should be able to recognize the piece and know how to play. (PI 566)

So the point of our using the same word 'pain' in both its first-personal and third-personal uses is that somebody will be able to pick up its use in one context (say, the third-personal) because he recognizes it as the word that occurs in another (say, the first-personal).

If one expunges from this suggestion the idea of a designing consciousness as connoted by the word 'purpose' one is left with a fairly plausible suggestion. The point is that we use the same word because someone who understands the word 'pain' in its first-personal context will, because of that use of it, *naturally* extend it to the third-personal context in such a way that he ascribes what he called 'pain' to other people on the grounds that we actually have for doing so (though for all that he is not logically compelled to do so). That is: the extended 'similarity space' that is centred upon our feelings of pain is such that we are more likely to extend our word for these feelings to people who are injured or cry out than we are to those who exhibit other types of behaviour.

This is an interesting empirical conjecture that cannot be settled in the armchair; if confirmed it would indicate one reason that one might have for regarding the use of the same word in first- and third-personal cases *neither* as forced upon us by the nature of things *nor* as a logically undesirable accident. Rather, the facts about how we extend the uses of words that have been taught to us in some limited sphere would be one of those 'facts of nature' by which we explain the formation of the associated concept (PI p. 195/230).

4.2.7. 'God sees it'

There is a very general objection to Wittgenstein's procedure here, one that applies not only at this point but also to his discussion of language-games, family resemblance, reading, understanding and meaning. That is because it latches onto a feature of the method of *Philosophical Investigations* that runs through the whole work and which distinguishes its approach very sharply from that in the *Tractatus*.

If somebody wanted to know the meaning of a sentence like 'Jones was reading at such-and-such time' we have seen how Wittgenstein would respond. He would offer an account of when we are *justified* in saying that he was reading. We are justified in saying it when he has said the written words right (i.e.) 50 times consecutively (PI 157). In the recently introduced terminology we can say that his doing so is a criterion for his reading.

Again, we can be *justified* in saying that somebody who gives the order 'Write down the sequence +2' means the sequence +2 and not some deviation from it. What justifies it is what he counts as 'obeying the rule' and 'going against it' in actual cases (PI 201). We may say that this too is a *criterion* of what he meant by the order.

And the same pattern is evident in his account of third-personal sensation ascriptions. The account tells us what justifies such ascriptions, that is, their criteria. In the case of pain, these are behavioural, but they need not be so long as they are 'outer'. For instance, there might be a sensation for which the criterion was a physiological event, such as a rise in blood pressure (PI 270).

In all of these cases we are not told the *truth*-conditions of the statements in question. We are only told when we are *justified* in making them. Contrast statements whose truth-conditions we *do* give. A statement of the form *x is a square* is true just in case *x*'s replacement denotes something that *has four equal sides that meet at right angles*. We are here being told what claim upon reality the statement, that something is square, makes. And this is just what his later accounts of reading, meaning, understanding, and third-personal sensation ascriptions appear to avoid.

We have already seen that in the *Tractatus* the statement of truth-conditions was the one and only way to explain a proposition: for the essence of the proposition is to lay a claim upon reality, to say that *this is how things stand* (TLP 4.5). It should also be evident that the Cartesian account of third-personal sensation ascriptions meets this demand. On that account you can explain to me the meaning of 'Johnny is in pain' to me by saying, 'You surely know what it is for you to be in pain. "Johnny is in pain" means simply that he has what you have when you are in pain' (cf. PI 350). Whatever the deficiencies of this account it at least *aspires* to that Tractarian ideal; that is, it attempts to specify what it would take for Johnny to *be* in pain, not just the sort of thing that would *justify* my saying so. Whereas the account that we are now considering does nothing of the sort: it makes it appear as though somebody who was able to recognize pain-behaviour knew all that there was to know about the meaning of 'Johnny is in pain'.

Well, it may be said, there is nothing particularly surprising or objectionable about that. The whole point of *Philosophical Investigations* was to break the spell of a highly unified conception of language, on which the analysis of a sentence conforms in all cases to a single ideal. When the spell is broken we see that there are indeed *many different* kinds of meaningful sentence, so too many different kinds of *explanation* of a sentence's meaning. Why then should anyone be surprised or concerned that the correct explanation of 'Johnny is in pain' is so different in form from that of 'Such-and-such is square'?

The answer – and this is the objection – is that *logic itself* seems to dictate otherwise. 'Either he is in pain or he isn't' is an instance of the theorem of classical logic known as the law of excluded middle; so is 'Either he was reading that first word or he wasn't' (recall the example at PI 157); so is 'Either he meant +2 or he didn't'. And it seems that the application of the law in these cases shows that there is more to the ascription of reading, meaning, understanding and pain than Wittgenstein allows. For the law seems to demand that there *be* a fact one way or another, even if *we* don't know what it is. *We* have to rely on these external signs of pain, or understanding; but the statement itself reaches into a hidden region of reality that in any case makes it *true* or makes it *false*.

But nothing in Wittgenstein's explanations of these statements shows what sort of fact this could be: all it tells us is what justifies us in those cases in which we *can* tell one way or another whether, for example, he is in pain. Wittgenstein's account therefore seems superficial. It seems that logic itself forces upon us a conception of these statements' meaning that is beyond the reach of the sort of explanation that he would have us accept.

In two passages, one of great beauty, Wittgenstein gives powerful expression to this concern.

> Here it happens that our thinking plays us a queer trick. We want, that is, to quote the law of excluded middle and to say: "Either such an image is in his mind, or it is not; there is no third possibility!" (PI 352)

> A picture is conjured up which seems to fix the sense *unambiguously*. The actual use, compared with that suggested by the picture, seems like something muddied. Here again we get the same thing as in set theory: the form of expression we use seems to have been designed for a god, who knows what we cannot know; he sees the whole of each of those infinite series and he sees into human consciousness. For us, of course, these forms of expression are like pontificals which we may put on, but cannot do much with, since we lack the effective power that would give these vestments meaning and purpose.

> In the actual use of expressions we make detours, we go by side roads. We see the straight highway before us, but of course we cannot use it, because it is permanently closed. (PI 426)

This passage also contains the seeds of Wittgenstein's reply. We must distinguish between the logical law itself, which is simply a convention of our language, and the *picture* that it suggested to us. The picture is of a region of reality that outruns its visible

WITTGENSTEIN'S *PHILOSOPHICAL INVESTIGATIONS*

part: the inside of someone's mind, say, or the infinite continuation of the decimal expansion of π. But that picture is *just* a picture: *it* tells us nothing about the actual use of the expression but just stands there like an irrelevant or merely ornamental illustration to a text.

Thus PI 352 continues:

> The law of excluded middle says here: It must either look like this, or like that. So it really – and this is a truism – says nothing at all, but gives us a picture. And the problem ought now to be: does reality accord with the picture or not? And this picture *seems* to determine what we have to do, what to look for, and how – but it does not do so, just because we do not know how it is to be applied . . .
>
> Similarly when it is said "Either he has this experience, or not" – what primarily occurs to us is a picture which by itself seems to make the sense of the expressions *unmistakable*: "Now you know what is in question" – we should like to say. And that is precisely what it does not tell him.[31]

The metaphysical *picture*, of a region of reality that outruns its visible part, is inert: once it is distinguished from the law of excluded middle it makes no difference to anything that anyone actually says whether or not we 'accept' that picture. So we should – of course – accept the law itself; but we should not think that *it* reveals any incoherence in the way we actually employ third-personal sensation ascriptions, which is what Wittgenstein takes himself to be describing.

Nor does this mean that the law of excluded middle should itself become an object of philosophical scrutiny, as though philosophers could settle whether or not it is true, in cases where the evidence is equivocal, that *either Jones was in pain or he wasn't*. To do so would be to have some independent means of deciding whether 'Jones was in pain' is either true or false in cases where I have no means of telling which. But there *is* no independent means for deciding that. Given Wittgenstein's conception of truth, 'It is true that Jones was in pain or it is false that Jones was in pain' is just another way of saying 'Either

Jones was in pain or he wasn't' and so cannot itself be evaluated by some prior method (cf. PI 136a, discussed at 2.4). 'Philosophy simply puts everything before us, and neither explains nor deduces anything' (PI 126). We have seen some reasons for dissatisfaction with that general attitude at 2.3. But given Wittgenstein's conception of truth its application to the present objection is entirely appropriate.

CHAPTER 4

RECEPTION AND INFLUENCE

Since its publication in 1953 *Philosophical Investigations* has been widely recognized as a great work. Strawson's review called it 'a treatment, by a philosopher of genius, of a number of intricate problems, intricately connected' (1954: 22), and Feyerabend wrote that considered as a contribution to traditional philosophy – rather than as a criticism of that enterprise – it was 'a great achievement' (1955: 149). More recently Michael Dummett has written that its first 100-odd sections 'almost all compel assent; although there may be large questions about how one should go on from there, it is almost impossible to read those paragraphs and maintain any reservations about this definitive treatment of the topics with which they deal' (1981: 239).

Its most notable early critic was Russell, who wrote that

> The late Wittgenstein . . . seems to have grown tired of serious thinking and to have invented a doctrine which would make such an activity unnecessary. I do not for one moment believe that the doctrine which has these lazy consequences is true. I realize, however, that I have an overpoweringly strong bias against it, for, if it is true, philosophy is, at best, a slight help to lexicographers, and at worst, an idle tea-table amusement. (Russell 1959: 216–17)

While it is easy to sympathize with Russell's puzzlement over why anybody who adhered to Wittgenstein's conception of philosophy would attach much importance to it, it is difficult not to consider this otherwise unfair. There is a good deal in *Philosophical Investigations* that makes a substantial contribution to our understanding of reality – and in particular the nature of thinking, meaning and understanding – while making none at all to lexicography. It is possible that Russell's judgement was biased by a lumping together of Wittgenstein with Ryle and the Oxford 'ordinary language' school under Austin (see Ayer 1984: 133–6).

Unlike the *Tractatus*, which from around 1925 dominated the thinking of that group of scientists and philosophers known as the Vienna Circle – whose members included Carnap, Schlick and Neurath – and which thereby – in consequence of the 1930s diaspora – had a deep if indirect influence on the positivist legacy in the United States, there was never any 'school' that drew its main inspiration from *Philosophical Investigations*. It did however exert a strong influence upon a number of individual philosophers; and, in the minds of those who were both insightful enough to absorb Wittgenstein's later philosophy and strong-minded enough not to find it overwhelming, it fostered some of the most original and important philosophical work since Wittgenstein's. Of these I shall mention three.[1]

Michael Dummett's work on logic and anti-realism proceeds from a Wittgensteinian premise among others. What he took from Wittgenstein was the idea that there can be no private semantic ingredient of a public language (see 4.1.3): if two individuals agree completely about the use to be made of a statement then they agree about its meaning (Dummett 1975a: 216, 226). He contended further that not *every* aspect of linguistic use was relevant to the meanings of the expressions involved; rather, some uses were so to speak definitive of those expressions: they laid down the meanings, and further patterns of use might be criticized for their infidelity to those meanings. In particular the patterns of inference that characterize classical logic were open to such criticisms: there is nothing in our overt application of 'true' and 'false' to simple mathematical statements that distinguishes those notions from the notions of proof and refutation; nothing, therefore, that justifies the further classical assumption that every statement is true or false; and so, finally, no justification (of the familiar truth-tabular sort) for the classical law of excluded middle (Dummett 1975a: 225–6).

We have seen that Wittgenstein himself would have rejected the idea that linguistic use was subject to criticism: it is for philosophers to *describe* linguistic use, not to criticize it. This difference between him and Dummett on this point can perhaps be traced back to Wittgenstein's insistence that the notion of truth has no content except as a device of disquotation (see 3.4). For if Wittgenstein had been right about that, it would have been futile in any case to demand any 'justification' of, for example, 'Either he was reading or he wasn't' in terms of the conditions under which its disjuncts were *true* (see 4.2.7). Of course Dummett rejects that 'redundancy' theory of truth (Dummett 1959: 4–7).

We have already had occasion to consider Kripke's seminal monograph (Kripke 1982) – probably the most influential work by an American philosopher to have been primarily inspired by *Philosophical Investigations*. In it Kripke develops a sweeping scepticism about meaning on the basis of the remarks on rule-following that we considered in Section 3. According to it there simply *is* no such thing as meaning, understanding, following a rule, and so on. But he also presents what he calls, following Hume, a 'sceptical solution to these doubts': it is still legitimate for us to *talk* about somebody's meaning one thing rather than another by his words. Only we must not think that in doing so we are describing any *facts*. The scepticism itself, though not the solution, has notable points of continuity with the work of W. V. Quine on the indeterminacy of translation and the inscrutability of reference. The main difference, as Kripke himself points out (1982: 57), is that Quine's arguments proceed on the *assumption* that no 'inner' processes can endow meaning upon otherwise meaningless signs; whereas among Wittgenstein's achievements are his arguments *for* this premise (see 3.3.2).

But we have also considered two differences between Kripke's presentation of Wittgenstein and what the latter actually wrote. It was of course Wittgenstein's view that there *are* such things as meaning and understanding and he was concerned only to combat certain misconceptions of them. More importantly Wittgenstein's conception of truth strongly suggests that he didn't think we could draw any line among assertions to separate those that do from those that do not 'state facts'; consequently he would have denied that there was anything sceptical after all about Kripke's 'sceptical solution' (see 3.4.2).

John McDowell's work deploys a number of recognizably Wittgensteinian ideas in a wholly different way, in particular certain strands of that 'romantic' side of his work which we had occasion to notice at PI 63–4 (see 1.3.4). Consider, for instance, the idea of exhibition at PI 201: we saw that you can exhibit your meaning to someone else, but he has to be someone who belongs to your community in the sense of sharing your natural reactions. McDowell's own epistemology is a development of this: on it, one can literally *hear*, for example, what somebody in one's own community is thinking (e.g. that he wants you to continue the sequence +2); whereas somebody *outside* of that community can not: 'shared membership in a linguistic community is not just a matter of matching in aspects of an exterior that we present to anyone whatever, but equips us to make our minds available to one another, by confronting one another with a different exterior from that which we present to outsiders' (McDowell 1984: 253).[2] And this is just one of many Wittgensteinian ideas that McDowell has taken up and developed in his own way; others include the private language argument and the Wittgensteinian conception of philosophy as an essentially reactive, not constructive, activity. McDowell 1994 is the fullest presentation of the resulting synthesis.

As these philosophers have illustrated Wittgenstein's later work has had a powerful and largely beneficial effect on the modern field; what they also illustrate to more varying degrees is that this effect is most likely to be achieved, not through slavish adherence to his own philosophical views or through an attempt to practice philosophy in the manner that he recommended, but through a critical engagement with those views in an attempt to discriminate and to extract whichever of his doctrines make a contribution to our philosophical knowledge. And that is the spirit in which you too should approach that work.

CHAPTER 5

GUIDE TO FURTHER READING

In addition to the works mentioned in the main text, the reader may find the following works helpful.

CONTEXT

The best short study of the *Tractatus* remains Ramsey's review of it (Ramsey 1923). But that is very difficult at a first reading. Mounce 1989 and Kenny 1975 are both excellent introductions.

SECTION 1. THE AUGUSTINIAN PICTURE

Baker and Hacker's monumental study of the *Investigations* combines section-by-section textual exegesis with scholarly essays on textual and philosophical questions raised by the text. A new edition of its first volume has recently been issued (Baker and Hacker 2004): chapter 1 of it is an excellent discussion of this material. Michael Luntley makes a very interesting case for an unorthodox reading of Wittgenstein's attitude towards Augustine: see his forthcoming and the references therein.

SECTION 2. FAMILY RESEMBLANCE AND THE IDEAL OF PRECISION

Bambrough 1960–1961 is an attempt to apply Wittgenstein's doctrine of family resemblance to the problem of universals. Forster (forthcoming) is a thorough and insightful critical study of Wittgenstein's discussion. Wittgenstein's doubts about the very possibility of philosophy, doubts that I have isolated from my interpretation of the rest of the work, are for some commentators its interpretative key. I have largely ignored this kind of reading because I do not consider it suitable for an introduction of this sort. But Stern 2004 is an excellent, sensitive reading of *Philosophical Investigations* in this 'Pyrrhonian' light.

SECTION 3. MEANING AND UNDERSTANDING

Heal 1989 chapter 9 discusses Wittgenstein's views on proof and meaning, as does Wright 1980 (which is as much a work on Dummett's views as it is on Wittgenstein's). Miller and Wright 2002 is a helpful collection of essays on Kripke's work on rule-following.

SECTION 4. PRIVACY

The 'Postscript' to Kripke 1982 contains lucid discussion of Wittgenstein's views on other minds. The last 15 pages of BB contain helpful discussion of Wittgenstein's views on the self; and his 'Notes for a Lecture on Private Experience and Sense Data', available in PO, contain very helpful background to the 'Private Language Argument'.

NOTES

1. CONTEXT

1 A note on the text. References in which 'PI' precedes a number are to *section numbers* of Part I of *Philosophical Investigations*. An occasional succeeding letter indicates a paragraph within a section; thus 'PI 1d' refers to the fourth paragraph of section 1. I have used the third edition. The pagination in that edition is slightly different from earlier editions, so if I refer to a page number in the third edition (which will happen when I want to refer to a remark in Part II or a note in Part I) I also mention the corresponding page in the first edition (1953), which matches that in the second edition.

It will soon become evident to anyone who reads it that at least some of the sentences in PI do not express the views or attitudes of Wittgenstein himself but those of an imaginary 'interlocutor'. Where the context does not make it clear I will use square brackets to indicate the quoted sentences of which this is true.

References to the *Tractatus* will also be by section number. As with references to *Philosophical Investigations* a succeeding letter indicates a paragraph within a section.

3. READING THE TEXT

1 'Causes and effects' is my crude interpretation of 'language and the actions into which it is woven' (PI 7d).
2 The reader will notice that Wittgenstein mentions exceptions to this rule and may be curious to know which ones he allowed. *One* sort of exceptional case is that in which the meaning of a word is said to be something that you experience (so that, for example, if you repeat a word enough times it starts to 'sound meaningless'). Wittgenstein discusses cases of this sort at PI pp. 182–5/214–17. PI does not make clear what the other exceptions are supposed to be.
3 Wittgenstein discusses a similar case at PI p. 160/187. There he says:

If you trained someone to emit a particular sound at the sight of something red, another at the sight of something yellow, and so on for other colours, still he would not yet be describing objects by their colours. Though he might be a help to us in giving a description. A description is a representation of a distribution in spaces (in that of time, for instance).

But this looks dogmatic. At any rate no reason is given for denying it the status of a report on *something*; or for denying that the whole – ostensive teaching plus consequent habitual response – is *some* kind of language-game.

4 This is roughly the account of ostension in Quine 1969: 121–4.

5 Someone might object that I have failed to distinguish what Wittgenstein calls 'ostensive *definition*' from what he calls 'ostensive *teaching*' (PI 6b). The form of training that I have described in connection with animals is only ostensive teaching; what distinguishes an occasion of ostensive definition is that the pupil is able to *ask the name* of the thing or type of thing that is then being defined. So all that my example shows is that ostensive teaching does not presuppose that the pupil can already speak a language; but what Wittgenstein aimed to establish was the weaker thesis that ostensive definition presupposes this.

   My two related replies are (a) that if we make it part of the definition of ostensive definition that the pupil be able to ask something's name then of course it will be true that 'I gave X a successful ostensive definition of "red"' entails 'X could already speak a language'. But if *this* is all that Wittgenstein had aimed to show then his argument loses all of its interest; (b) that neither Augustine nor any of the empiricists who might reasonably be taken to be targets at this point have relied upon any such distinction: for them, the idea that ostension lay at the bottom of language was the idea that ostensive teaching did so. (Augustine nowhere speaks of *asking* his elders the names of the objects before him.) In short the distinction between ostensive teaching and ostensive definition can only save Wittgenstein's argument at the cost of making it irrelevant.

6 For further discussion of this *Notebooks* material see Sullivan 2003.

7 It is true that in the written version of the language they have the letter 'a' in common, but this is not something of semantic significance in the manner of (say) the ending 'o' in 'Ambulo'. In the *Tractatus* it is our *meaningful use* of signs that turns them from semantically inert to semantically significant elements of language – what he there called 'symbols'. See TLP 3.262, 3.326–3.328.

8 See, for example, the illuminating discussion of why we call facial features 'friendly' at BB 145.

9 PI 78 is puzzling in this connection, for in its comparison of *how the word 'game' is used* with *how a clarinet sounds* it appears to be suggesting that both are things that one can know *without* being able to say them. On the criterion of 'being able to say' that is operative in the text that seems to be simply wrong – though evidently on that criterion one can only say how the word 'game' is used to the right kind of audience. See further 3.4.3.

10 See also the helpful discussion in Fogelin 1987: 133–4.

11 Of course I'd also apply it ('wrongly') to *all* cuboids, parallelepipeds, and so on, but this makes no difference to the present point.

12 For further discussion see Hacker 1999; Stern 1995: 67–9.

13 Cf. Evans's remark on this 'deep conceptual prejudice' – Evans 1980: 276–7.

14 Wittgenstein does immediately concede that 'observation of regular concomitances is not the only way to establish causation.' He may have had in mind Russell's discussion in 'The Limits of Empiricism'. See Rhees's note to 'Cause and Effect: Intuitive Awareness' in PO p. 370.

15 Isn't it wrong to call 'thinking of the formula' an *experience*? Wittgenstein has already shown (see 1.2) that there is no experience of 'attending to the shape' or 'attending to the colour'. Couldn't he argue similarly that there is none of 'thinking of the formula'? – And indeed he does seem to endorse a similar view of what happens when one thinks of a *person* (PI 691).

I think that in this passage he *must* mean 'thinking of the formula' to denote a type of experience. Otherwise the fourth sentence of PI 179, which speaks explicitly of such an experience, would be quite irrelevant. And I think that he avoids any inconsistency because when he speaks in *this* passage of 'thinking of the formula' he just means, for example, that B has a *mental image* of the *sign* for the formula (or for that matter an 'outer' experience of that sign). This would explain his interpolation of the words 'saying it, writing it down' in the quoted passage.

16 Kripke's own, somewhat confusing, discussion of PI 136a is at p. 86; I discuss it in Ahmed 2007: 142–6.

17 For instance it would apply to one's knowledge of the ABC (PI 149).

18 He takes a comparable attitude towards other forms of scepticism, for example, that about other minds (PI 284, 288–9, 303), induction (PI 472) and the external world (OC 369–71).

19 Locke himself falls short of being ideally Lockean in this respect. At *Essay* II.xxxii.15 he says that there are *many* reasons for thinking that other people feel the same chromatic sensation as I do when, for example, we look at a marigold: 'but that being besides my present Business, I shall not trouble my reader with them'.

20 For instance at PI 256 he writes: 'But suppose I didn't have any natural expression for the sensation, but only had the sensation? And now I simply *associate* names with sensations and use these names in descriptions.' And at PI 257 he writes: ' "What would it be like if human beings shewed no outward signs of pain (did not groan, grimace, etc.)? Then it would be impossible to teach a child the use of the word 'tooth-ache'." – Well, let's assume the child is a genius and himself invents a name for the sensation!'

21 Two further objections might seem to apply at this point.

The first point is that merely saying 'cow' in the (visible) presence of cows is not enough to make 'cow' denote cows because it faces an underdetermination problem: to say 'cow' in the visible presence of a cow is to say 'cow' in the visible presence of the surface of a cow. So what makes it true that 'cow' refers to cows rather than to their surfaces? I reply that *every* language-game, however complex, faces an equally devastating underdetermination problem. The private diarist faces no special difficulty here.

The second point is directed against my claim that if somebody who is engaged in as simple a language-game as the builders can be said to have names for her instruments, then so can the private diarist. The difference between the builders and the private diarist, it will be claimed, is that B has other responses to 'Slab!' than just the mechanical fetching of a slab. It may be, for instance, that B will shake her head if she sees nothing slablike in the vicinity, and shrug her shoulders if she sees, for example, items that *might* be slabs but might equally be beams.

But there is no reason why the private diarist should not play a similarly complicated language-game. It may be, for instance, that he writes 'S' in his diary-entries for days on which he definitely did not have S. And it might be that the boundaries of the type are indefinite, so that his behaviour is like that of someone whose use of an inner sample is as described at PI 73. In that case he may, for example, write 'S?' in his diary to describe days on which he experienced a borderline case.

22 See also Blackburn 1984: 299–300.
23 Notable among these are Wright 1986, Canfield 2001 – and of course Kripke 1982, which however places no special emphasis on PI 258, arguing instead that it is simply a special case of a more general argument that had already been made by PI 202 (Kripke 1982: 3).
24 Note that *that* precise meaning for 'same public use' is what makes the first premise – that a permutation of the inner objects associated with our public words is immaterial to their public use – very strong; but it is also what makes this second premise very weak. And PI 293b does in fact establish that strong first premise; that is why I said that the present interpretation of 'same public use' gives Wittgenstein's argument the best possible chance.
25 This term is usually reserved for Quine's doctrine, best stated by him at 1968: 28–9: '[T]here are no meanings, nor likenesses nor distinctions of meaning, beyond what are implicit in people's dispositions to overt behaviour.' As long as the two are not confused there is no harm in appropriating the term in the present context; doing so also highlights the closeness between the two philosophers on this point.
26 Here I sketch a version of the argument at Quine 1981: 19–20.
27 At this point it may be worth mentioning Frege's argument that if everyone's words referred to his private ideas then there could be no verbal expression of a dispute between two people. Frege's view seems to have been that if you say 'Nettles are always green' and I say 'Nettles are not always green', and if we each mean some different private sensation-type by 'green', then we are not really disagreeing any more than two people are disputing whether

a ten-pound note is genuine, 'where each meant the one he himself had in his pocket and understood the word "genuine" in his own particular sense' (Frege 1967: 29). But it suffices for genuine disagreement between two parties that there be sufficient *agreement* between them as to what sorts of evidence would settle the truth-value of the disputed sentence. More generally the fact that disputants refer with the same words to different things does not forestall their framing disagreements in a public language: for instance, a nominalist mathematician could certainly express disagreement with a Platonist one over a mathematical theorem stated in the usual terms.

28 The treatment of solipsism in the *Tractatus* – to which the quoted passages belong – is notoriously difficult and its interpretation highly contentious. The present interpretation of it is based upon Kripke's reading, for more details of which see Kripke 1982: 131–2 n. 13.

29 You might retort that in that case the place where I felt it counts in virtue of just that fact as part of 'my body'. But then we can retort back that in *that* case the claim that 'I' refers to my body is equivalent to the tautology that 'I' in 'I feel such-and-such' refers to *whatever it is that feels something when I feel it*; but to say that that is 'what "I" refers to' is not to say *anything* about what 'I' refers to.

30 This is not the only interpretation of Wittgenstein's term; its most prominent rival (McDowell's) differs from it on just this point. See McDowell 1982, esp. p. 380.

31 McDowell 1978: 303 n. 16 is a helpful commentary on this passage.

4. RECEPTION AND INFLUENCE

1 These are certainly not the only three philosophers of whom this is true. Among the most important of the remainder is G. E. M. Anscombe, whose seminal *Intention* (1957) applied Wittgensteinian insights to problems to do with intention, action, decision and the will.

2 The connection with the romantic idea of a national character is obvious. Contrast Hume: 'Would you know the sentiments, inclinations and course of life of the Greeks and the Romans? Study well the temper and actions of the French and the English: You cannot be much mistaken in transferring to the former most of the observations which you have made with regard to the latter.'

REFERENCES

WORKS BY WITTGENSTEIN

BB   *The Blue and Brown Books.* Oxford: Blackwell, 1960.
LFM   *Lectures on the Foundations of Mathematics: Cambridge 1939.* Ed. Cora Diamond. Chicago: University of Chicago Press, 1975.
NB   *Notebooks 1914–16.* Ed. G. E. M. Anscombe and G. H. von Wright, trans. G. E. M. Anscombe. Second edition. Chicago: University of Chicago Press, 1984.
OC   *On Certainty.* Ed. G. E. M. Anscombe and G. H. von Wright, trans. G. E. M. Anscombe and D. Paul. Oxford: Blackwell, 1969.
PI   *Philosophical Investigations.* Ed. G. E. M. Anscombe and R. Rhees, trans. G. E. M. Anscombe. Third edition. Oxford: Blackwell, 2001.
PO   *Philosophical Occasions 1912–1951.* Ed. J. Klagge and A. Nordmann. Indianapolis: Hackett, 1993.
RFM   *Remarks on the Foundations of Mathematics.* Ed. G. E. M. Anscombe, R. Rhees and G. H. von Wright, trans. G. E. M. Anscombe. Oxford: Blackwell, 1991.
TLP   *Tractatus Logico-Philosophicus.* Trans. D. F. Pears and B. F. McGuinness. London: Routledge, 1961.
Z   *Zettel.* Ed. G. E. M. Anscombe and G. H. von Wright, trans. G. E. M. Anscombe. Second edition. Oxford: Blackwell, 1981.

OTHER WORKS

Ahmed, A. 2007. *Saul Kripke.* London: Continuum.
Ayer, A. J. 1954. 'Could there be a private language?' *Proceedings of the Aristotelian Society*, Supplementary vol. 28: 63–76. Reprinted in G. Pitcher, ed., *Wittgenstein: The Philosophical Investigations*: 251–66. London: Macmillan.
—. 1971. *Language, Truth and Logic.* Second edition. Harmondsworth: Penguin.
—. 1984. *Wittgenstein.* Harmondsworth: Penguin.
Baker, G. P. and Hacker, P. M. S. 2004. *Wittgenstein: Understanding and Meaning. Part I: Essays.* Oxford: Blackwell.
Bambrough, R. 1960–1961. 'Universals and family resemblances'. *Proceedings of the Aristotelian Society* 61: 207–22.
Blackburn, S. 1984. 'The individual strikes back'. *Synthese* 58: 281–301.
Canfield, J. V. 2001. 'Private language: The diary case'. *Australasian Journal of Philosophy* 79: 377–94.

Carnap, R. 2003. *The Logical Structure of the World*. La Salle, Ill.: Open Court.

Craig, E. J. 1997. 'Meaning and privacy'. In R. Hale and C. Wright, eds, *Blackwell Companion to the Philosophy of Language*: 127–45. Oxford: Blackwell.

Dummett, M. A. E. 1959. 'Truth'. *Proceedings of the Aristotelian Society* 59: 141–62. Reprinted in his *Truth and Other Enigmas* (1978): 1–24. London: Duckworth.

—. 1975a. 'The philosophical basis of intuitionistic logic'. In H. E. Rose and J. C. Shepherdson, eds, *Logic Colloquium '73*: 5–40. Amsterdam: North-Holland. Reprinted in his *Truth and Other Enigmas* (1978): 215–47. London: Duckworth.

—.1975b. 'Wang's paradox'. *Synthese* 30: 301–24. Reprinted in his *Truth and Other Enigmas* (1978). London: Duckworth.

—. 1981. Frege and Wittgenstein. In I. Block, ed., *Perspectives on the Philosophy of Wittgenstein*: 31–42. Oxford: Oxford University Press. Reprinted in his *Frege and Other Philosophers* (1991): 237–48. Oxford: Clarendon Press.

Evans, G. 1980. 'Things without the mind'. In Z. van Straaten, ed., *Philosophical Subjects: Essays Presented to P. F. Strawson*: 76–116. Oxford: Clarendon Press. Reprinted in his *Collected Papers* (1985): 249–90. Oxford: Oxford University Press.

Feyerabend, P. 1955. 'Wittgenstein's *Philosophical Investigations*'. *Philosophical Review* 64: 449–83. Reprinted in G. Pitcher, ed., *Wittgenstein: The Philosophical Investigations*: 104–50. London: Macmillan.

Fogelin, R. 1987. *Wittgenstein*. Second edition. London: Routledge.

Forster, M. Forthcoming. 'Wittgenstein on family resemblance concepts'. In A. Ahmed, ed., *Wittgenstein's Philosophical Investigations: A Critical Guide*. Cambridge: Cambridge University Press.

Frege, G. 1967. 'The thought: A logical enquiry'. Trans. A. M. and M. Quinton, in P. F. Strawson, ed., *Philosophical Logic*: 17–38.

Frege [1892] 1960. 'On sense and reference'. In P. Geach and M. Black, eds, *Translations from the Philosophical Writings of Gottlob Frege*: 56–78. Oxford: Blackwell.

Glock, H.-J. 1996. *A Wittgenstein Dictionary*. Oxford: Blackwell.

Hacker, P. M. S. 1999. 'Naming, thinking and meaning in the *Tractatus*'. *Philosophical Investigations* 22 (2): 119–35.

Heal, J. 1989. *Fact and Meaning: Quine and Wittgenstein on Philosophy of Language*. Oxford: Blackwell.

Hume, D. [1739] 1949. *Treatise of Human Nature*. Ed. with an analytical index by L. A, Selby-Bigge. Oxford: Clarendon Press.

Kenny, A. J. P. 1975. *Wittgenstein*. Harmondsworth: Penguin.

Kripke, S. A. 1982. *Wittgenstein on Rules and Private Language*. Oxford: Blackwell.

Locke, J. [1694] 1979. *Essay Concerning Human Understanding*. Ed. P. H. Nidditch. Oxford: Clarendon Press.

Luntley, M. Forthcoming. 'What's doing? Activity, naming and Wittgenstein's response to Augustine'. In A. Ahmed, ed.,

Wittgenstein's Philosophical Investigations: A Critical Guide.
Cambridge: Cambridge University Press.

McDowell, J. 1978. 'On "The reality of the past"'. In C. Hookway
and P. Pettit, eds, *Action and Interpretation: Studies in the Philosophy
of the Social Sciences*: 127–44. Cambridge: Cambridge University
Press. Reprinted in his *Meaning, Knowledge and Reality* (1998):
295–313. Harvard: Harvard University Press.

—. 1982. 'Criteria, defeasibility and knowledge'. *Proceedings of the
British Academy* 68: 455–79. Reprinted in his *Meaning, Knowledge
and Reality* (1998): 369–94. Harvard: Harvard University Press.

—. 1984. 'Wittgenstein on following a rule'. *Synthese* 58: 325–63.
Reprinted in his *Mind, Value and Reality* (1998): 221–62. Harvard:
Harvard University Press.

—. 1994. *Mind and World*. Harvard: Harvard University Press.

McGinn, M. 1997. *Wittgenstein and the Philosophical Investigations*.
London: Routledge.

Malcolm, N. 1954. 'Wittgenstein's *Philosophical Investigations*'. *Philosophical Review* 63: 530–59. Reprinted in G. Pitcher, ed., *Wittgenstein:
The Philosophical Investigations*: 65–103. London: Macmillan.

Miller, A. and C. Wright, eds. 2002. *Rule-Following and Meaning*.
London: Acumen.

Moran, R. 2003. *Authority and Estrangement*. Princeton: Princeton
University Press.

Mounce 1989. *Wittgenstein's Tractatus: An Introduction*. Chicago:
Chicago University Press.

Quine, W. V. 1968. 'Ontological relativity'. *Journal of Philosophy* 65:
185–212. Reprinted in *Ontological Relativity and Other Essays* (1969):
26–68. New York: Columbia University Press

—. 1969. 'Natural kinds'. In N. Rescher, ed., *Essays in Honour of Carl
G. Hempel*: 5–23. Dordrecht: Reidel. Reprinted in *Ontological
Relativity and Other Essays* (1969): 114–38. New York: Columbia
University Press.

—. 1981. 'Things and their place in theories'. In his *Theories and Things*:
1–23. Harvard: Harvard University Press.

Ramsey, F. P. 1923. 'Critical notice of the *Tractatus*'. *Mind* 32: 465–78.

Russell, B. [1912] 2001. *The Problems of Philosophy*. Oxford: Oxford
University Press.

—. 1959. *My Philosophical Development*. Woking: Unwin.

Stern, D. 1995. *Wittgenstein on Mind and Language*. Oxford: Oxford
University Press.

—. 2004. *Wittgenstein's Philosophical Investigations: An Introduction*.
Cambridge: Cambridge University Press.

Strawson, P. F. 1954. 'Review of Wittgenstein's *Philosophical Investigations*'. *Mind* 63: 70–99. Reprinted in G. Pitcher, ed., *Wittgenstein: The
Philosophical Investigations*: 22–64. London: Macmillan.

Stroud, B. 2001. 'Private objects, physical objects and ostension'.
In D. Charles and W. Child, eds, *Wittgensteinian Themes: Essays in
Honour of David Pears*: 143–62. Oxford: Oxford University Press.

REFERENCES

Sullivan, P. 2003. 'Simplicity and analysis in early Wittgenstein'. *European Journal of Philosophy* 11: 72–88.
Wright, C. 1980. *Wittgenstein on the Foundations of Mathematics*. London: Duckworth.
——. 1986. 'Does *Philosophical Investigations* I, 258 suggest a cogent argument against private language?' In J. McDowell and P. Pettit, eds, *Subject, Thought and Context*. New York: Oxford University Press.

INDEX

acquaintance (Russellian) 1–3,
  6, 9
Ahmed, A. 158n. 16
analysis 3, 4, 12, 24–2, 29, 31–5,
  47–51
Anscombe, G. E. M. 160n. 1
anti-realism 151
Aristotle 66
assumption 31
Ayer, A. J. 116

Baker, G. P. 154
Bambrough, R. 154
'bank' 143–4
'beetle-in-the-box' 121–8
Berkeley, G. 66
'Bismarck' 90–1
Blackburn, S. 159n. 22
blood pressure 145
The Blue and Brown Books
  (BB) 67, 70, 77, 155
brain 78–9, 82–4, 129–30

calculations 63
Canfield, J. V. 159n. 23
Carnap, R. 107, 151
Cartesian picture, the 129–30,
  139, 141
causal connection 23, 89–91, 97
chromatic words 20, 28, 54,
  56–7, 108, 122–3
complement 127
compositeness 26, 34, 36–7, 45
Confessions (St Augustine) 11
context principle (Frege) 5
contradiction 55–6
Craig, E. J. 109

criteria 139–41
  vs. symptoms 140–1
cube, the 70

decision 12, 98
derivation 86–8
Descartes, R. 129–30, 134
  see also Cartesian picture
descriptions, Russell's theory
  of 2–4
dispositions 76–84
duck-rabbit 57
Dummett, M. A. E. 55, 150, 152

Einstein, A. 66
epistemic asymmetry, the 130–4
Evans, G. 22, 158n. 13
excluded middle, the law
  of 146–51
exhibit 101–3, 153
experience
  of attending to something 18–19
  of being influenced 91
  of guidance 86, 90, 92
  of meaning something 156n. 2
  of the self 90

facts 72, 75, 99
family resemblance 8, 19, 40–7,
  51, 69, 87–8, 92, 145, 154
  and vagueness 45–7
Feyerabend, P. 150
fitting 69, 73–5
Fogelin, R. 157n. 10
Forster, M. 154
Frege, G. 1, 4, 53–4, 159n. 27
functional unity 12, 39

reference 15, 23, 111, 124, 152
referentialism 22–34
  in ordinary language 23–4
  simplicity and
    compositeness 26–9
  in the *Tractatus* 24–34
*Remarks on the Foundations of
  Mathematics* (RFM) 33,
  56, 75, 90
Rhees, R. 158n. 14, 161
rule-following 107
Russell, B. 1–2, 5, 9, 49,
  66, 150

St Augustine 11, 16, 157n. 5
Augustinian picture 11–40, 54
scepticism 101, 134, 152
Schlick, M. 151
'seeing as' 58
self, the 134–7
semantic behaviourism 127–8,
  159n. 25
sensation 111, 120–1, 130
  first-personal avowals 138
  third-personal
    ascriptions 137–45
sense 3–10, 13, 31–2
  vs. reference 3, 4
sense data 2
sepia 28–9
sequence, numerical 80, 95, 106
set theory 147
similarity space 120, 144
simplicity 26–9
Socrates 34
Sorites (sequence) 54, 55, 100
sortalism 113, 118–19
spirit 40
Stern, D. 154, 157n. 12
Strawson, P. F. 114–15, 150
Stroud, B. 119
Sullivan, P. 157n. 6

Sun, 5 o'clock on it 139
symptoms 140–1

Tractatus Logico-Philosophicus
  (TLP) 1, 3–9, 11–12,
  24–41, 43–5, 48–9, 58,
  60–3, 67–9, 72, 91, 135,
  142–3, 145–6, 151, 154,
  157n. 7
objects 3, 6, 9, 24–6
picture theory
  (of meaning) 6, 36
propositional forms 67–9
solipsism in 160n. 28
symbol 72, 157n. 7
  vs. sign 72, 135, 143
syntax 62
types, theory of 61
tricolor 33, 47
truth 8, 66, 68, 100, 148–9, 152
truth-conditions 4, 31, 41, 48, 60,
  145–6

understanding 69
  grasping in a flash 69–70
  and guidance 84–94
universals 2, 3, 27, 154
use
  meaning as 18, 30, 69–70
  public use 125

vagueness 45–51, 57, 88
  and analysis 47–51
verificationism 113, 118

water 77–8, 80
will 91, 160n. 1
Wright, C. 155, 159n. 23, 162–4

yellow ochre 56

Zettel (Z) 83